"It's so hard to balance love and discipline, when our kids are making poor choices. But *Bonding with Your Teen through Boundaries* makes it a lot easier. With a 'how-to' practicality, June Hunt helps parents tackle the hardest problems their kids face on the road to adulthood."

Josh McDowell, author & speaker

"June Hunt's clear wisdom accumulated through two decades of interactive talk radio exudes through every page of this wonderful and much-needed book. Twenty-first century teenagers are crying for the fruit of this message. The discerning parent who reads and applies the wisdom found herein will undoubtedly save their kids from hurt, tears, and potential destruction."

Joe White, President, Kanakuk Kamps

"If teens are a part of your life, you now hold in your hands the *real* answers to the *real* challenges you will face. Each practical chapter spells out 'what you can do' and 'what you can say'—not to win a battle, but to win a *relationship* of mutual respect. A *must read* for anyone who deals with teens— whether yours, or someone else's."

Marlene Wright, Probation Officer, Johnson County, Texas

"Teenagers don't always make wise choices. However, as *Bonding with Your Teen through Boundaries* points out, wrong behavior offers their parents many opportunities to provide loving correction and guidance. Thanks to June and Jody for this practical guidebook—filled with timeless principles from God's Word—to help navigate many of the greatest challenges parents face."

Brian S. Simmons, President, Association of Christian Schools International

"As someone who has worked with teenagers for over forty years, June sets a tone in teenage discipline that I had to learn through experience. She shows us the proper balance between our God-given mandate to train our children as they grow into self-managed adults and the loving relationship we want with them. Abounding with truth, wisdom, and practicality, this is important reading for parents and anyone else who works with teenagers."

Jason Stevenson, Pastor of Student Ministries, Stonebriar Community Church

"June Hunt is well qualified to address the issue of bonding with your teen through boundaries. On her radio show, *Hope for the Heart,* she has encouraged literally thousands of parents to become the kind of parents God wants them to be. I highly recommend this well-thought-out book to be read by every parent."

Dawson McAllister, author, speaker, & host of
Dawson McAllister Live

"We are grateful for the practical teaching of June Hunt. Her decades-long ministry and personal experiences make her a very qualified guide for parents of teenagers. Any who desire to keep connected to their teens as well as help them navigate their bumpy road will be grateful for June Hunt."

Steve Douglass, President, Campus Crusade for Christ International

BONDING WITH YOUR TEEN
THROUGH BOUNDARIES

BONDING

with your **TEEN** through

BOUNDARIES

JUNE HUNT *with* **JODY CAPEHART**

REVISED EDITION

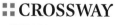

CROSSWAY

WHEATON, ILLINOIS

Bonding with Your Teen through Boundaries

Revised edition, copyright © 2010 by Hope for the Heart, Inc.

Published by Crossway
        1300 Crescent Street
        Wheaton, Illinois 60187

Originally published by B&H, 2001.

Cover design: Amy Bristow

First printing, 2010

Printed in the United States of America

Italics in biblical quotes indicate emphasis added.

Unless otherwise indicated, Scripture quotations are from the ESV® Bible (*The Holy Bible, English Standard Version*®), copyright © 2001 by Crossway. Used by permission. All rights reserved.

Scripture references marked AMPLIFIED are from *The Amplified Bible, Old Testament*, copyright © 1965, 1987 by the Zondervan Corporation. Used by permission.

Scripture quotations marked MESSAGE are from *The Message*. Copyright © by Eugene H. Peterson 1993, 1994, 1995, 1996, 2000, 2001, 2002. Used by permission of NavPress Publishing Group.

Scripture quotations marked NASB are from *The New American Standard Bible*®. Copyright © by The Lockman Foundation 1960, 1962, 1963, 1968, 1971, 1972, 1973, 1975, 1977, 1995. Used by permission.

Scripture references marked NEB are from *The New English Bible*, © by The Delegates of the Oxford University Press and The Syndics of the Cambridge University Press, 1961, 1970.

Scripture indicated as from NIV is taken from *The Holy Bible, New International Version*®. Copyright © 1973, 1978, 1984 by Biblica. Used by permission of Zondervan. All rights reserved. The "NIV" and "New International Version" trademarks are registered in the United States Patent and Trademark Office by Biblica. Use of either trademark requires the permission of Biblica.

Scripture references marked NLT are from *The Holy Bible, New Living Translation*, copyright © 1996, 2004. Used by permission of Tyndale House Publishers, Inc., Wheaton, Ill., 60189. All rights reserved.

ISBN-13: 978-1-4335-1620-7
ISBN-10: 1-4335-1620-9
PDF ISBN: 978-1-4335-1626-9
Mobipocket ISBN: 978-1-4335-1627-6
ePub ISBN: 978-1-4335-1628-3

Library of Congress Cataloging-in-Publication Data
Hunt, June.
   Bonding with your teen through boundaries. — Rev. ed. /
June Hunt with Jody Capehart.
     p. cm.
Includes bibliographical references.
   ISBN 978-1-4335-1620-7 (tpb)
   1. Parent and teenager. 2. Parent and teenager—Religious aspects—
Christianity. 3. Parenting. 4. Discipline of children. I. Capehart, Jody.
II. Title.
HQ799.15.H86   2010
248.8'45—dc22   2010009038

Crossway is a publishing ministry of Good News Publishers.

VP			19	18	17	16	15	14	13	12	11	10
14	13	12	11	10	9	8	7	6	5	4	3	2	1

This book is dedicated to the delightfully endearing,
fun-filled young people in my life—my nieces and nephews:

Ashlee, Heather, Henry, Hunter I,
Hunter II, Josh, Kathryn, Kimberly, Leah,
Lillian, Mara, Tanner, Teddy, and Travis.

My prayer is that you will always be young in spirit,
pure in heart, and right with God.

Contents

SECTION IV
Personal Boundaries

SECTION V
Social Boundaries

Acknowledgments

I have deepest gratitude to the team who worked together like true Super Bowl champs.

Bonding with Your Teen through Boundaries was first released in 2001, the same week as 9/11—the radical Islamic terrorist attacks on United States soil. With national attention riveted on the unfolding tragedy, efforts to promote the book would have been insensitive and unproductive. As a result, the release came . . . and went . . . largely unheralded.

Since 2001, the need for biblical, practical, relevant help for raising teenagers has grown more pressing in view of the deteriorating culture. As a result, the second edition of this book, released in 2010, offers many new chapters and thoroughly updated information throughout.

As a team, our great privilege and prayer is to help you be all that God created you to be . . . and to help you help others.

Barbara Spruill and *Trudie Jackson* presented the game plan from their years of working with teens and continued coaching until the last second of the game. Without them, there would be no book.

Robin Hardy and *June Page* ran with the game plan during the first half. *Jody Capehart* then took over during the second half—writing and updating the material to make sure the contents were unquestionably current.

Connie Steindorf and *Angie White*—quarter after quarter—ran with blazing fingers across their computer keyboards.

Carolyn White, Titus O'Bryant, Bea Garner, Elizabeth Gaston, and *Jeanne Sloan* made sure the ball wasn't dropped in the fourth quarter.

Beth Stapleton and *Karen Williams* together, with bleary eyes, proofed the book across the end line as the game clock ran out.

What a joy to see this team running . . . filled with seamless, selfless synergy. Together as one we can truly say, "I run in the path of your commands, for you have set my heart free" (Ps. 119:32 NIV).

SECTION I

What Are Boundaries All About?

1

Prepare Your Kite for Flight

Teenagers are a hot topic. One writer lamented, "They now seem to love luxury and have bad manners and contempt for authority. They show disrespect for adults and spend their time hanging around places gossiping with one another. They are ready to contradict their parents, monopolize the conversation and company, eat gluttonously and tyrannize their teachers." Not much has changed since Socrates made these complaints some twenty-four hundred years ago!

Immediately after college I became intimately acquainted with those turbulent teenage years—the time of tremendous change—as a youth director in a large downtown church. I had six hundred in the junior high division, grades seven, eight, and nine. It didn't take long to learn that between ages thirteen and sixteen teenagers came in like lambs and went out like lions! I not only marveled at the changes but also gained invaluable insights. Many of those practical insights are shared within the pages of this book.

For example, in the earliest years of your child's life, you as a parent represented God—and I mean that literally. You represented total authority. You were always right. Then your teenager entered into a time of "individualization"—that fifty-dollar word describing the stage of development when children strive to become independent young persons. No longer do they simply accept your morals, values, and teachings based on "because I said so!"

Teenagers need—and actually want—to choose for themselves how they will respond to rules, or else they could find themselves sliding down a dangerous, slippery slope. That is why Proverbs 4:14–16 gives this clear caution: "Do not enter the path of the wicked, and do not walk in the way of the evil. Avoid it; do not go on it; turn away from it and pass on. For they cannot sleep unless they have done wrong; they are robbed of sleep unless they have made someone stumble."

What Are Boundaries All About?

If teenagers don't heed this warning, they will end up following *anyone* at *any time* for *any reason*—especially any so-called authority who comes along with a message that sounds good . . . whether it be a drug dealer, cult leader, or gang lord.

Unfortunately for parents, this new push for independence is not usually a gradual transition. Your kids hit the teen years, and PRESTO CHANGE-O!—all of a sudden Mom knows nothing and Dad is a dinosaur. Their attitude is: "My parents must have been born in the Stone Age!"

During this time of tug-of-war, teenagers will test you, tempt you, and try you. In other words, they will try to see whether there are any *real* rules. Many parents become baffled by their teens' behavior, thinking, *What happened to my submissive son? Who is this difficult daughter? How do I deal with this awful attitude?*

If something similar is happening in your home, take heart: *Now is not forever.* One day you may be surprised to see that your teenagers have grown to be appreciative adults who finally hear your heart and see your sacrifices. Until that time, however, establish the rules, enforce them each time, endure to the end, and be sure to *hold on to hope.*

In a way, kids are like kites. (I'm fully aware that some adults object to using the word *kid* for a young person because *kid* literally means a young goat. However, I affectionately use the word *kid* as a term of endearment—probably because it's casual, and kids like most things to be casual.)

Speaking of kites and kids, I can still picture a large Thanksgiving gathering at my mother's home some years back. When I walked outside, I noticed a kite on the ground, a kite obviously discarded in frustration. The string was knotted into a huge, oddly shaped ball. A few relatives joined me in wanting to fly the kite, but we didn't have any other string. So for twenty minutes or more, three of us stood around the kite untangling the knots one at a time.

The process was slow and tedious. But when the tangles were untied, the kite was put to flight. At first it ascended into the air, eliciting our smiles, laughter, and cheers. It then abruptly descended in a nosedive and hit the ground. That downfall, however, did not dash our hopes. After several more unsuccessful launches, the kite again was put to flight—and oh, how it soared!

Just because many teens have their lives all tied up in knots doesn't mean they should be treated like discards. Just because they've fallen to the ground doesn't mean they are hopelessly defeated. Untangling a mess takes persistence and patience. Be encouraged by this compassionate principle from the Bible: "A man's wisdom gives him patience; it is to his glory to overlook an offense" (Prov. 19:11 NIV).

To be the best parent possible, you must have persistence and patience while being empowered by God and guided by the right goal.

A PARENT'S HIGHEST GOAL

Our ultimate goal as parents is to prepare our "kites" for flight so they can be all that the "Kite Maker" intended. Simply put: *Prepare your child to live independently of you, yet dependent on God, successfully soaring with self-control.* This self-control will not be misdirected when it is grounded by the Word of God, governed by the Son of God, and guided by the Spirit of God.

By God's design you have been placed in a key position to prepare your kite for flight. How?

FOUR KEY POINTS—FOR KITES *AND* KIDS

1. Kites need open spaces in order to soar. They will be hindered by hovering tree limbs. As a parent, be open with your teen and don't hover.
2. Kites need to be attached to a firmly held ball of string. They will plummet to the ground if you let go completely. As a parent, don't let go of your teens. Even when they make it difficult, stay connected. Keep holding on, giving them love—keep holding on, giving them limits.
3. Kites need the string to be gradually released more and more in order to soar higher and higher. As your kids take on increased responsibility, don't fear giving them increased freedom.
4. Kites need balance. The weight of the tail balances the kite, keeping it from flip-flopping. If you find yourself being accused of weighing your teenager down, don't despair—your teenager needs *balance through boundaries.*

If you really care about your kids, learn how to present boundaries with both repercussions and rewards. Teenagers will be far more balanced with boundaries, and in the end you will delight in seeing them soar!

2

The Black Hat

To the fascination of the watching world, the early 1900s ushered in the first motion pictures, in black and white. Western films were popular fare as the two main characters—the hero and the villain—shot it out with their six-shooters or fought it out with their fists.

In the old Westerns, it didn't take any time at all to discover which was the *good guy* and which was the *bad guy.* The good guy always wore the white hat. The bad guy always wore the black hat. Everyone liked the hero in the white hat. No one liked the villain in the black hat.

WHO WANTS TO WEAR THE BLACK HAT?

And so it goes in the family. No parent wants to be the villain—no dad wants to be disliked, and no mom wants to be disrespected. Every parent wants to be liked and listened to with respect. So what do you do when your teenager deliberately disobeys and you don't want to be perceived as a villain wearing "the black hat"?

Some parents assume the solution is *permissiveness*: permit kids to do whatever they want (often against a parent's better judgment) so they won't get upset and the family can live in peace. For kids who cross the lines, no reprimand, no reproach, no repercussion.

But this passive peace-at-any-price approach won't reap the positive results you desire. You need to raise a self-disciplined teenager who respects your role as a parent and your right to set the rules.

WASN'T JESUS A PEACE-AT-ANY-PRICE PERSON?

Many people—Christians and non-Christians alike—think "peace at any price" is the Christian way to live. *After all,* they reason, *Jesus is called the Prince of Peace.* They even quote Jesus' words, "My peace I give to you"[1] and "Blessed are the peacemakers."[2] The apostle Paul even said, "If it is possible, as far as it depends on you, live at peace with everyone."[3]

In light of these biblical passages, we need to ask ourselves, was Jesus a peace-at-any-price person? By no means. Instead he countered this common misconception by pronouncing, "I did not come to bring peace, but a sword."[4] Jesus clearly communicated that he must confront what is wrong by cutting to the heart of the matter. He announced, "The truth will set you free."[5]

The sword of truth is necessary to live a life of integrity and to confront needed changes when nothing around you is peaceful. If you do what is right in His sight, Jesus gives you His supernatural peace . . . an internal *peace that passes all understanding.*

How does this happen? When you receive Jesus Christ as your personal Lord and Savior, He comes in to take control of your heart and life. Because He is the Prince of Peace, *He will be your peace* in the midst of any storm—even a stormy time with your teenager. But having the peace of Christ on the inside is entirely different from being a peace-at-any-price person.

WHAT HAPPENS WHEN YOU ARE A PEACE-AT-ANY-PRICE PARENT?

Recently two young people told me their parents had been "too permissive." One fifteen-year-old confided, "My mother doesn't want to tell me *no*, so my stepfather gets mad at her because she backs down on the rules she sets for me."

Likewise, an attractive twenty-year-old admitted, "When I was much younger, I never should have been permitted to stay out so late . . . and I never should have been permitted to go out with certain men—they were much too old for me. My parents never checked on me. Now that I'm on my own, I've had real difficulties setting and keeping personal boundaries."

Both young people said they didn't think their parents cared enough about them . . . they were too busy, too preoccupied to set appropriate boundaries. And both admit they've acted angrily and disrespectfully toward their parents.

Ultimately, if you are too permissive, three primary problems surface:

1. They *disrespect* your appropriate rules.
2. They *dismiss* their need for self-discipline.
3. They *disregard* your role and your right to parent them.

In the end, you *decrease* your teens' respect for you.

So, what do you do? You know you shouldn't be a peace-at-any-price parent, but at the same time you don't want to go to war . . . you don't want to say *no* . . . you don't want your teen to put the *black hat* on you!

You must simply do this: you must learn the benefit of boundaries.

WHAT ARE BOUNDARIES?

Boundaries are *established limits*—lines not to be crossed. If a boundary is exceeded, the result is a *repercussion*. If a boundary is maintained, the result is a *reward*.

When a parent establishes a boundary, the teenager will choose to go beyond the boundary or stay within it. Realize, this means the teenager, not the parent, is the one who *chooses a repercussion* or a *reward*. This also means *the parent will not wear the black hat*!

One example of a *physical boundary* is the dividing lines drawn for the Olympic track-and-field events. In the 100-meter race—the rapid sprint that determines "the fastest man in the world"—all runners burst out of the starting blocks at the sound of the gun. If a runner steps into the lane of another runner, the *repercussion* is immediate disqualification. As long as all runners stay within their boundary lines, each reaps the *reward* of competing until the end of the race, with the very real possibility of winning the gold medal.

All sports lovers understand *athletic field boundaries*. In American football, the ball carrier who stays inside the sideline can advance the ball downfield with the hope of scoring. However, the play is called dead the instant the ball carrier's foot steps out of bounds . . . *across* the boundary line. Violators of the boundary line must pay the penalty.

At the Wimbledon championships, an entire tennis match can hinge on whether the ball lands within the boundary line or a fraction of an inch beyond it. In the sports world, boundaries are so important that technicians have perfected the slow-motion instant replay from different angles to discern whether the line has been crossed.

In the larger game of life, boundary lines exist in all areas of life. If you drive a car, you are bound by traffic lanes, stoplights, and speed limits. Ignoring these *motoring boundaries* can be fatal. Driving within them can save your life.

Behaviors have boundaries too—*ethical* or *moral boundaries*. At times legal boundaries overlap or coincide with moral boundaries that distinguish right from wrong. A prime example of both a moral and a legal boundary is theft. From 1932 to 1934 the infamous bank robbers Bonnie and Clyde went on a rampage of crime that included numerous robberies and killings.

Ultimately these notorious outlaws received the *punishment* their crimes warranted, both being killed in a massive shootout. Because Bonnie and Clyde crossed both the moral and legal boundaries of the land, they reaped the repercussion of death.

Many young people choose to live outside moral boundaries by engaging in promiscuous sex. They justify their actions by saying, "It's not against the law!" Nevertheless, they can experience the *repercussion* of sexually transmitted diseases (STDs), an unwanted pregnancy, or a sexual addiction.

What's more, when they cross *biblical boundaries*, they reap the repercussion of God's judgment . . . and His lack of blessing. However, teens who remain sexually pure until marriage need not fear STDs. They enjoy the *reward* of a clear conscience as well as God's blessing. And someday they can experience the purest relationship possible—pure oneness with their life partner.

WHAT DO YOU SAY TO TEENS WHO DON'T WANT BOUNDARIES?

Obviously teenagers want the freedom to do whatever they want. Yet imagine a clever young goldfish gurgling, "I don't like this glass bowl— it's keeping me from going where I want to go and doing what I want to do—it's too limiting! I want to get free of this bowl."

So one day the goldfish jumps a little here and leaps a little there. Finally, with the flip of his fins and a flap of his tail, he leaps outside the bowl. Now the fish is free! He's cleared the boundary of the bowl.

But now what happens to our little goldfish? Within minutes he dies. This one single act doomed him to certain death. Why?

1. Goldfish need water.
2. The fishbowl held the needed water.
3. The boundary of the bowl held the water the goldfish needed for life.

Being free to do whatever you want to do may *seem* right, but that doesn't make it right. As Proverbs 14:12 says, "There is a way that seems right to a man, but its end is the way to death." This is precisely why young people need their parents' guidance. That's why your teens need you to talk with them about boundaries and explain realistic repercussions and rewards.

WHAT IS THE PRIMARY BENEFIT OF BOUNDARIES?

External boundaries are designed to develop *internal* character. Read that line again! Teenagers experience an appropriate repercussion for defying a boundary, because a painful consequence is designed to develop discipline. Conversely, parents who let their kids continue getting away with wrong are *training them to do wrong*.

For example, parents who let a daughter experience no repercussion for being disrespectful toward them are training their daughter to be disrespectful toward other authority figures. Likewise, she doesn't learn self-discipline. Truthfully, is this in her best interest? Obviously not. A lack of discipline in adolescence won't prepare her for the discipline she'll need in adulthood.

What happens if your son repeatedly reaps *no repercussion* for coming home *after curfew*? You are training him to disrespect time. Years later, when he tries to keep a job, he has no discipline to meet his scheduled deadlines. He has trouble being on time because he was not *trained* to respect time. This is *not* preparing your kite for flight. This is *not* disentangling your son so he can soar with self-control.

A short time ago, on a flight from California to Dallas, I sat beside a college freshman. During our conversation I asked, "Did your parents ever give you boundaries?"

"Oh yes," he quickly answered.

"Did they enforce them?"

"Oh yes," he replied again with more emotion. "Last year my parents set a midnight curfew for Friday and Saturday nights. Well, one night I let the time slip by, not taking the curfew that seriously. I came in at 2:00, and that was it! My parents refused to let me drive my car for two weeks."

"What impact did that have on you?"

"It was awful," he moaned. "Every day for the next two weeks I had to ask somebody to drive to my house and take me to school, and someone else to drive me home after school. I also had to get rides to and from any activities away from school. I couldn't do anything for myself."

"Did that repercussion make any difference in your life?"

"You bet it did—whenever I was out late, I watched my watch like a hawk!"

"Did you feel your parents were unloving?"

"No, there's no question they love me. In fact, I know my parents did what they did *because* they love me." He spoke with absolute assurance.

"Did you feel that the repercussion was excessive in any way?"

"Oh, I thought it was excessive at the time. But that's what all kids think when a strict consequence is enforced. Today I see how the difficulty of being without my car helped me become much more time-conscious. The fact that I had to pay a penalty for being irresponsible helped me to be much more responsible. Now that I'm on my own at Texas A&M, I'm thankful for what my parents did—and I think they're great!"

Perhaps the moral of this true story could be summarized this way: To teens, these parents may appear to wear the black hat, but one day they'll see the black hat turn white!

Additional related resources (audio and print) are available from Hope for the Heart (http://www.hopefortheheart.org/):

Decision Making

3

Understanding Your Teen

"I don't have time to wash the car. Anyway, I don't feel like it." "No way am I going to some little kid's birthday party—I don't care what his dad did for you." "I'll go see whatever movie I want!" "Quit nagging me! . . . I don't have to do what you say. And don't forget, I need you to wash my jeans." *Ouch.*

Your son has developed a real attitude problem. He argues with you about everything. He's defiant, disrespectful, and definitely disagreeable. A year ago he was such a wonderful boy. Who is this person . . . this adolescent . . . this teenager?

Being a parent of a teen is no easy task. The range of emotions for teenagers is vast, and their developmental needs are daunting. Being a teenager is challenging as well. On any given day a teen will wrestle with doubts and questions regarding almost every area of life. One such question might be: "Why do people tell me these are the best years of my life? Is this as good as it will ever get?"

A TIME OF TRANSITION

Adolescence is a time of transition. Teenagers are transitioning from childhood to adulthood, and *change* is the *one constant* in their lives. (The Latin word for adolescence is *adolescere*, which means "to grow up."[1])

Physically, teenagers are:

- developing sooner than previous generations,
- experiencing hormonal and sexual changes, and
- needing at least eight to nine hours of sleep a night.

Emotionally, teenagers are:

- living in the "now" and giving no thought to future consequences,

- acting positively and compliant one minute, arguing and resisting authority the next minute, and
- feeling indestructible and immortal.

Mentally, teenagers are:

- increasing in ability to learn, reason, and solve problems,
- seeking novelty and making creative choices, and
- multitasking with electronics while studying and engaging in other activities.

Socially, teenagers are:

- transitioning dependence from parents to peers,
- wanting to feel connected to others, and
- searching for *love, significance,* and *security.*

Spiritually, teenagers are:

- questioning what faith in God means on a personal level,
- needing an authentic relationship with the Lord Jesus Christ, and
- wanting to establish their own personal convictions.

Developmentally, the fact that your teen's brain differs from your adult brain helps explain why teens and parents typically have different responses to the same situation.

- The *prefrontal cortex* is directly behind the forehead and is responsible for organization, impulse control, and planning. This area is the logical, reflective part of the brain. Adults generally function from this part of the brain, whereas in teens this area is still developing.
- Teens generally function from the *amygdala*, the emotion center of the brain, a fact that helps explain why they are often impulsive and short-tempered and view life events differently than their parents.
- The *hypothalamus* regulates hormones within the body and is a major player since teens' hormones affect much of their development.

Other processes occurring in a teenager's brain provide a window of opportunity to *learn things quickly* and with more ease. Additionally, a human being's sensitivity for addiction is never stronger than during the teen years.

"Adolescent brains get the gas before the brakes. The brain's gas pedal is ready for a NASCAR-paced adulthood. But because the PFC [prefrontal cortex] is not up to snuff, the brain's got the brakes of a Model T."[2] At a time when teenagers desire to be *self-directed*, they still need to be *parent-directed*.

WHAT COULD YOU DO?

On a positive note, with your teens' ability to learn quickly and their desire for novelty, consider taking them on missions trips or finding other ways of involving them in ministries where they can learn and serve others.

Rather than allowing them to feed the potential for addiction with electronic entertainment, drugs, sex, or alcohol, expose them to the many needs of the world and let them experience being a part of meeting these needs firsthand. Instill in them a biblical worldview. Encourage their dependence on God and the development of an appetite for His Word.

In the midst of your teens' instability, you can provide needed relief by having clearly defined and firmly established values, expectations, and convictions in regard to your teens. Your confidence will be a healing balm to their insecurity and your steadfastness a safety net for their instability.

Verify your values, establish your expectations, and confirm your convictions in the following areas:

- *Academics*: What kind of grades do you expect from your teens? Are they solely responsible for their homework?
- *Spiritual life*: Do you engage your teens in spiritual instruction and conversation as well as urging consistent church attendance?
- *Social life*: What kind of curfew do you set? Where can they go, and with whom?
- *Behavior*: Do you allow disrespect, disobedience, or dishonesty? What is acceptable and what is unacceptable?
- *Character*: What traits do you want developed in your teens? What are you doing to help develop them?
- *Possessions*: How tidy must your teen's room be? Do your teens have a dress code?
- *Entertainment*: What do you let your teens watch on TV and on videos? What about movies and concerts?
- *Responsibilities*: What chores do you expect your teens to do? Do you provide accountability?
- *Privileges*: Who pays for extracurricular activities? Who pays for transportation?
- *Family life*: What are your expectations for family time? Have you defined your own boundaries as a parent?
    — Expect respect because it's the right thing and not just "because I said so."

— Reward positive behavior with your affirmations and not with money.

— Your goal is to build inner qualities in your teens.

Don't rescue your teens when you should establish repercussions.

• Rescuing weakens character and sets teens up to establish relationships with people who will further enable their irresponsible choices.

• Repercussions provide opportunities to learn lessons, retrain the brain, and cultivate Christlike character.

Be your teens' parent, not their buddy.

• If they get in trouble at school, don't automatically blame the school. Hold teens accountable, if warranted.

• If they don't get their homework done, don't do it for them. Let them suffer the repercussions—they need to experience repercussions.

Write a letter of encouragement to each of your teens expressing how you feel about him or her.

• Take your time. A letter is an investment in your relationship that will last a lifetime.

• Keep it positive. Here are a few suggestions to help you start:

> Dear . . .
> I want you to know how much I love you.
> The day you were born was one of the greatest, most awesome days in my life.
> I remember . . . .
> One of my favorite things about you is . . . .
> One of my best memories of time with you is . . . .
> You're so good at . . . .
> I'll always be here for you.
> I believe in you.

WHAT COULD YOU SAY?

The clouds of angry, sullen attitudes from teenagers often make it difficult to see any light at the end of the tunnel regarding your relationship. How can you clear the clouds of negative teenage attitudes to see what is really going on with teens? How can you keep the communication lines open in order to keep the real issues the main focus?

Use the "Sandwich Method" to confront and correct:

FIGURE 3-1

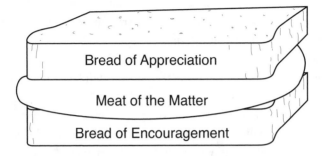

Bread of Appreciation

Meat of the Matter

Bread of Encouragement

1. Begin with the "Bread of Appreciation." Mention an internal character trait, not external looks or talents. *"I really appreciate your (perseverance)..."* Proverbs 16:21 says, "The wise in heart are called discerning, and pleasant words promote instruction" (NIV).
2. Add the "Meat of the Matter" by stating the problem. *"Because I love you/care about you, I want you to realize..."* Proverbs 9:9 and 12:1 say, "Give instruction to a wise man, and he will be still wiser; teach a righteous man, and he will increase in learning.... Whoever loves discipline loves knowledge, but he who hates reproof is stupid."
3. Finish with the "Bread of Encouragement"—*"I know when you really apply yourself, you will succeed."* First Thessalonians 5:11 says, "Therefore encourage one another and build one another up, just as you are doing."

In response to the rollercoaster emotions of kids, don't emotionally react to their immaturity or you'll find yourself in a vicious cycle of one emotional outburst after another. Instead take charge of your impulse control and clearly state in an emotionally detached way what you expect from your teenager. Understand you are *not* to detach from your teens—you are to be emotionally detached from what was inappropriately said and done. The Bible says there is "a time to keep silence, and a time to speak" (Eccles. 3:7).

Likewise, since you have every right to expect respect from your teens, state your expectations and what repercussions will follow if they are not met. "If you choose to talk this way to me, not only will your jeans not get washed, but you will not be going anywhere to wear them. Let me know when you are ready to speak respectfully to me." Proverbs 13:13 (NIV) says, "He who scorns instruction will pay for it, but he who respects a command is rewarded".

If your teens fail to put the brakes on but keep pressing you and wanting to argue, then you can say, "Unless you stop right now, your actions will result in having specific privileges withdrawn. This sincerely is not *my* choice, but *your choice.* If you choose to continue to speak disrespectfully, then *you are making that decision for me.* Are you willing to have numerous privileges withdrawn? It is ultimately up to you."

You need to make it clear that all privileges—taking the car, going on dates, attending parties, even using the phone—will be on hold until they can respectfully talk to you.

If back talk continues after you've made your position clear on a particular issue, you will not only have to put all privileges on hold but cancel previously planned activities as well. Consider Hebrews 12:9: "We have had earthly fathers who disciplined us and we respected them."

If your teenager was verbally abusive, then an apology is due to you. Even if it's insincere, saying the words may be a needed lesson in humility. You can't make people repent in their hearts, but your gentle insistence that they acknowledge their wrongdoings can be used by the Spirit of God to convict them privately later. Carefully read and write out Proverbs 6:2–5.

There is no greater gift you can give your teens than your time and unconditional love. Yes, your teens are busy, and so are you. But they want you to take time from your busyness and show them you care, that you're there for them. They want to hear the words, "You matter to me. I love you." The greatest boundary against disrespectful attitudes and actions is the boundary of love.

Talkative teenagers can be a blessing or a curse, depending on the talk that comes out of their mouths. As you gain mastery over your own words, speak words that build up your teenagers. Perhaps everyone could put this Scripture on their bathroom mirrors and be reminded of this instruction:

WISDOM FROM GOD'S WORD

Let no corrupting talk come out of your mouths, but only such as is good for building up, as fits the occasion, that it may give grace to those who hear. (Eph. 4:29)

Additional related resources (audio and print) are available from Hope for the Heart (http://www.hopefortheheart.org/):

Parenting; Rejection; Teenagers; Mentoring

4

Questions and Answers about Boundaries

Fireworks can produce spectacular sights that delight and excite. Fireworks also can produce dangerous explosions that misfire and maim. In the context of family relationships, if you as a parent wait to establish boundaries until your children are teens, your entire family could experience explosive "fireworks."

Every successful parent knows that boundaries are essential to battle a culture that states, "There are no moral absolutes." Even though you have your teenager's best interests at heart, boundaries can ignite caustic attacks from your teen. Verbal assaults can explode all over you and other members of your family. This may cause you to doubt whether you should have even set boundaries in the first place and whether you are willing to maintain them.

Questions about boundaries are common among parents, and they need to be addressed. If you settle the questions now, you need not be mentally attacked with self-doubt when you are in the heat of battle, when you need confidence to stand your ground. The Bible says, "Do not throw away your confidence, which has a great reward. For you have need of endurance, so that when you have done the will of God you may receive what is promised" (Heb.10:35–36). Confidence in these verses refers to confidence in Jesus as our Savior, but that confidence also feeds our confidence in handling life situations, including parenting.

IS IT REALLY NECESSARY TO IMPOSE BOUNDARIES ON TEENAGERS?

Yes. But as a parent, you are *imparting* boundaries, not *imposing* them. Realize that if your children grow up without boundaries, they will feel

31

frustrated and possibly frightened because of insecurity within their own lives. In one fascinating sociological study, researchers took a group of young children and placed them in a large open field to play. There were no fences or boundaries for miles. The researchers then watched the children from a hidden location. For the most part, the children huddled close together, playing rather fearfully.

The researchers then took them to a large field bounded by tall, chain-link fencing on all sides and let them play on their own. The children wandered all over the field to the far corners of the fencing and played with much greater confidence. Ultimately the discipline of boundaries will produce in your young people a sense of safety, security, and confidence in decision making.

As a parent, knowing your children are secure in who they are brings peace to your soul. The Bible says, "Discipline your son, and he will give you rest; he will give delight to your heart" (Prov. 29:17).

WON'T BOUNDARIES LIMIT MY TEENAGER'S CREATIVITY?

No. Boundaries establish a safe structure that will enhance your teenager's creativity. God created the world with natural boundaries, such as gravity. Without that boundary we would not be able to live on the earth He created. Almost everything would be floating in space! In the same vein, He created people with behavioral boundaries—foremost among them the Ten Commandments given in Exodus chapter 20—so we can live in harmony with God and with one another.

Life without these moral boundaries, where people are free to murder or steal, causes chaos. Living within these moral boundaries provides God's peace and builds good moral character. Moral boundaries also help protect your teenager from needlessly stumbling. The Bible says, "Great peace have those who love your law; nothing can make them stumble" (Ps. 119:165).

When teens feel the safety net of defined boundaries enveloped in unconditional love, their creativity will abound. Their developmental energy can be used to find out who they are (identity), what their skills are (significance), and how loved they are (security).

32

AREN'T TEENAGERS TOO OLD FOR PARENTAL DISCIPLINE?

No. Boundaries help aim and direct you toward a target. Your target is to train your teenager to become internally motivated to do what is right. In reality, no one outgrows the need for guidelines and accountability, but teenagers do outgrow certain methods of discipline. Many parents, motivated by love, spank their younger children. However, spanking a teenager is not only ineffective but can create serious repercussions in the form of rebellion and alienation.

The purpose of this book is to help you explore methods of discipline that are appropriate and practical with teens. In a similar way, the apostle Paul recognized the need for encouraging those closest to him, those who were under his care: "You know how, like a father with his children, we exhorted each one of you and encouraged you and charged you to walk in a manner worthy of God, who calls you into his own kingdom and glory" (1 Thess. 2:11–12).

CAN BOUNDARIES REDUCE TEEN STRESS?

Yes. Without realizing it, teens may become overcommitted. Usually the problem begins with adding one activity on top of another until they never have a moment to relax. Some teen suicides have resulted from feelings of never quite measuring up—or even catching up. Activities may provide wonderful experiences for your teens, but the *cumulative* effect of them may increase stress.

Carefully look at your teens' schedules and the amount of sleep they are getting. Teens need eight hours of sleep a night because of the way their bodies are growing and changing. If your teens are going to bed but talking/texting on the phone, watching television, or surfing the Internet instead of sleeping, some boundaries need to be established. You may meet with initial resistance, but as your teens begin to feel the benefits of getting enough sleep, the resistance will diminish.

Talk with your teens about these issues, and involve them in finding the solution. Teens often have great ideas. When they are part of the solution, they often accept more responsibility.

WHAT ARE STEPS TO SUCCESS WHEN SETTING BOUNDARIES WITH TEENS?

The purpose of boundaries is to create a climate conducive for the development of Christlike character in your teens. Boundaries are to be positive, proactive, and mutually respectful. Boundaries help teens make correct choices and assume responsibility for their choices. Successful boundary building will include:

Step 1: Communicating with Them

- Dialogue with your teens regarding what each of you needs from the other, and establish specific expectations based on those identified needs.
- Write down everyone's expectations and sign the documented agreement as an acknowledgment that everyone understands and commits to honoring the newly established boundaries.

Step 2: Giving Them Unconditional Love

- Assure your teens that even though you will not always like what they do, you will always love and value them.
- Communicate your unconditional love on a daily basis even if your teens do not respond or reciprocate.

Step 3: Showing Them Respect

- Respect is a two-way street; so show respect for your teens if you want them to show respect for you.
- Accept your teens' right and need for dignity by knocking on their door before entering their rooms, by allowing them to speak without interruption, and by listening attentively to what they say and how they feel.

Step 4: Empowering Them

- Instill in them the belief that they can make a positive difference in the lives of others and in their own circumstances.
- Encourage them to make more and more choices as they demonstrate their ability to keep boundaries.

Step 5: Spending Time with Them

- Spend time collectively and separately with your teens in order to establish a foundation for boundaries and to enjoy and get to know them better.

- Work with your teens to plan meaningful outings and activities. Encourage their input.

Step 6: Listening to Them

- Be attentive and contemplative, listening with your heart and asking yourself, "What are my teens *really* saying?"
- Be patient with your teens, who are aching to be heard but don't always know how to express their thoughts and feelings.

Step 7: Accommodating Them When Necessary

- Realize that your teens' behaviors simply reflect where they are developmentally—their brains respond emotionally rather than rationally—and realize that when your teens say, "I hate my life. I hate you. I wish I had never been born," what they are really saying is, "I'm confused. . . . I'm frustrated. . . . I've messed things up. . . . I wonder if I am lovable. . . . Help!"
- Evaluate the reasons your teens give for violating boundaries, refusing to make excuses for them or to accept lame excuses from them. Change boundaries that are ineffective.

Step 8: Praying for Them without Ceasing

- Pray that the boundaries you establish for your teens will be based on God's truths and that your own beliefs and behaviors don't violate a boundary set by God.
- Pray that your communication *and* convictions will be held captive to the obedience of Christ.

HOW CAN I ENFORCE BOUNDARIES WITHOUT SEEMING CRUEL?

Make sure your teens know that you take no pleasure in ruining their day. Take care to comment on the positive character traits you have noticed. Also remember God's purposes for proper discipline. Boundaries are not just external limits with negative repercussions. *The goal of a good boundary is to teach self-control, which in turn develops godly character. Along with that godly character comes a solid, inner moral compass that always directs a person toward making a godly decision.* If you do your job as a parent by enforcing discipline at the proper time, your teens may not vote you "The Most Popular Parent of the Year." But just wait a while—the

Bible says, "For the moment all discipline seems painful rather than pleasant, but later it yields the peaceful fruit of righteousness to those who have been trained by it" (Heb. 12:11).

IS THERE SUCH A THING AS A BAD BOUNDARY?

Yes. Some boundaries may be either too restrictive or too lenient for the age and maturity level of teens. A parent who insists that high school students be home by 10:00 PM on a Friday night from a school event that isn't even over until 10:00 is being too restrictive. On the other hand, a parent who sets a curfew of midnight on a school night for a high school activity over at 10:00 is being too lenient.

A group of high school students being interviewed about what makes a "good" parent and what constitutes a "bad" parent gave quick and consistent responses. A "good" parent is one who is strict, follows through, and spends time with them. A "bad" parent is abusive, has no rules, and is unfair.

They all agreed that the *worst* parents are the ones who don't want to bother with you at all, those "who do whatever they need to do to get you out of their hair." These words spoke volumes. Teens want time and boundaries!

Frequent statements made by teens today attest to the fact that they often feel ignored because parents give them too much freedom and time alone.

With prayer and observation of your teens, you will be able to discern God's will for each specific situation. However, once you settle on a fair and just boundary, the repercussions as well as the rewards should be made clear and without apology. (Again, make sure the boundary is truly *just*.) The Bible gives this warning: "Fathers, do not provoke your children to anger, but bring them up in the discipline and instruction of the Lord" (Eph. 6:4).

WHAT ARE EXAMPLES OF APPROPRIATE BOUNDARIES?

- A parent tells a chronically late daughter, "We need to be on time for the dinner party. If you're ready when the car pulls out at six o'clock, we won't have to go without you." This communication principle is drawn from Proverbs 16:21: "The wise of heart is called discerning, and sweetness of speech increases persuasiveness."

- A parent tells an angry son, "I know you are angry, and I respect your feelings. But yelling and berating me reflects negatively on you. How you express your anger is *your* choice. What I will allow in my presence is *my* choice, and right now my choice is to leave for a while. I hope you will find a positive way of interacting so we can talk together calmly." This response is based on the Scripture, "A fool gives full vent to his anger, but a wise man keeps himself under control" (Prov. 29:11 NIV).
- A parent tells a demanding daughter, "I care about your needs and desires, but I need some time to think about what you are asking. We can talk about it tomorrow." Proverbs 19:2 warns us to think before acting: "Desire without knowledge is not good, and whoever makes haste with his feet misses his way."
- A parent tells an untrustworthy son, "I know you want me to trust you with the car again, and I want to reestablish that trust. For us to work toward that, I need at least one month your going only where you say you are going. That will show me you are serious about being trustworthy." Luke 16:10 confirms that someone who is faithful in the little things will be faithful in the big things: "One who is faithful in a very little is also faithful in much, and one who is dishonest in a very little is also dishonest in much."

More complex, in-depth examples of boundaries are included in the following chapters. Most of these examples come from letters to our ministry or from our radio programs. In both cases we draw from the wisdom of God's Word to address the dilemmas of life. The particular scenarios chosen for this book demonstrate how parents can defuse the teenage time bombs that often destroy family relationships and how parents can nurture their teenagers to maturity through the use of biblical boundaries.

First and foremost, pray that you will be the wisest parent possible—especially in the midst of "family fireworks." Why not begin each day with this prayer in your heart? "Teach me to do your will, for you are my God! Let your good Spirit lead me on level ground!" (Ps. 143:10).

Additional related resources (audio and print) are available from Hope for the Heart (http://www.hopefortheheart.org/):

Conflict Resolution

SECTION II

Boundaries at Home

It has been said, Home is where the heart is.

We all want home to be a place of peace—a refuge from the wrongs of the world—for everyone in the family. But if a teenager resides at home, it can become a battleground over rights and responsibilities. In order to have "home sweet home," boundaries are essential . . . not just for your teen's sake, but also for the sake of everyone else who must share the living space.

Your home is the training ground for boundaries. Home should be the place where you can lovingly but firmly train your teens to understand the important role they play as family members and how staying within the boundaries sets them up for success. Realize that in order to establish the best training ground for your teens and to have home sweet home, boundaries are not only needed—they are essential.

5

Back Talk

You've just walked out of the guest bedroom when you hear Lee open the front door.

"Whoa—hold up! Where are you going?"

"Over to Jessica's."

"Not now, honey. Your grandparents should be arriving any minute."

"Why do you always have to tell me what to do?"

(You're stunned. You know you are anything but a dictator!) You remind Lee that this dinner has been planned for months.

"This isn't a home—it's a prison!"

"Lee, your words are inappropriate!"

Then with raised right arm in mock salute and a "Heil Hitler," your testy teen abruptly turns and stomps back upstairs.

Why is your teenager acting like this? What is triggering these verbal bullets? Has he declared war on you?

Talking back is an equal opportunity practice used by both sexes, but with different styles. Boys and girls usually express themselves in predictable ways along gender lines.

In an attempt to manipulate, girls tend to cry, whine, throw temper tantrums, or use sarcasm. In an attempt to intimidate, boys might do the same things (except maybe cry), but with a confrontational, aggressive edge generally missing in a girl's delivery. This aggression calls for a different response. First, let's talk about girls.

WHAT COULD YOU DO?

A mother of two teens aged fifteen and thirteen relates this experience:

> My two girls had been sniping at each other. No matter what I said, they were rude to me and to each other. So I bought two tubes of travel-sized

toothpaste and left them on the dining room table. One of the girls asked why they were there. I replied nonchalantly that they were for an experiment we would get to later.

Finally, after four days, when one daughter asked again about the experiment, I gave both girls a saucer and a tube of toothpaste and told them to squeeze out as much toothpaste as they possibly could. Both got right to work, eyeballing each other's saucer to see who was getting the most out and who would finish first.

When they finished and looked at me expectantly, I said, "Okay, the *real* contest is to see who can get the most toothpaste *back* into the tube."

The older one began to try desperately, but the younger just pushed the saucer away saying, "That's impossible." After a moment I replied, "You're right. The same is true of words. Like toothpaste, once they come out, you can't get them back in."

I opened my Bible to James 3:10 and read, "From the same mouth come blessing and cursing. My brothers, these things ought not to be so." Then I left the table to cook dinner. No lectures, no pounding.

The next day when they began insulting each other, I started making distasteful faces. When they noticed my expression, I said, "That toothpaste tastes awful." They became quiet. They got the point! What a memorable way of breaking a bad habit.

While the previous illustration is about bickering between siblings, the "toothpaste" principle applies equally to back talking. Many times back talk is not habitual but situational; that is, talking back stems from a distressing situation—such as a deep disappointment or a painful rejection. Sometimes when an emotional situation erupts into tears or haranguing, the best course is to hold your peace and listen.

Be willing to overlook emotional accusations or wild threats—they are probably intended to get your attention or test your boundaries. More likely than not, they are your teen's feeble attempt to vent frustration, fear, hurt, or injustice.

Make certain you hear your child's distress call. Let your teenagers talk. Listen for content without judging delivery. Don't try to solve anything or answer questions unless specifically asked. Just listen for what is behind the reaction and for what is needed from you. Many times an attentive ear, an embrace, or an assurance of your love is all that is needed for young people to acquire a better frame of mind.

If defiance continues or becomes hostile, your teenagers could be developing real "smart mouths"—talking back to you, using sarcasm or even profanity on a regular basis. And although your teens may eventually comply with your instructions, it seems that almost every request you make is met with disrespect or a hostile verbal response.

Since undesirable behavior is sometimes extinguished by simply ignoring it, you might first try that approach. As long as your teens ultimately do what you have requested and are not making obscene or vile comments to you, in the strictest sense of the word you are being obeyed. Remember to pick your battles, and don't mistake blanks for bullets. That is, teenagers frequently say things they don't mean, either to dramatize their point or just to see how you will respond.

Don't take everything they say to heart. And whatever you do, *don't shoot back*. That's the equivalent to fighting fire with gasoline. If you stoop to that level, they will throw it back in your face.

If your teenagers do say something hurtful and you are truly grieved, you could take a deep breath . . . speaking slowly and softly. "Is that what you really mean to say?" Seeing that you are hurt by their words could appeal to their consciences. Seeing your pain might give them a moment to reflect on what they really want to say. Keep in mind that they are not your enemies, and you do not want them to see you as their enemy. You are meant to be allies in the battle that rages within them to win their independence without disrespecting or dishonoring you.

If ignoring the disagreeable talk is not effective, then set the simple but firm rule: "When I say, 'end of discussion,' it means there will be no further comments without the repercussion of withdrawn privileges or additional assigned work around the house." Then walk away.

Language that was utterly taboo for the general public a few years ago is now widely heard, especially in the media. Profanity has become such an accepted form of expression in our culture that you should not be shocked if your teens try it with you. It doesn't mean they're hopeless degenerates.

Teenagers frequently use expressions whose original meanings are completely unknown to them. One mother who found a note a girl had written to her fourteen-year-old son explained, "I was shocked at the extremely coarse language, especially coming from a girl! But it was also sadly ironic in that she completely misspelled a number of the offensive words."

This is not to say coarse language should be tolerated from your teenagers. It shouldn't. If any profanity is uttered in your presence, make it clear that such language could mean the end of their social contacts for a while. "I can't have you talk that way. You know that profanity is unacceptable in our home. So tonight you won't be talking to anyone other than yourself and God." Then immediately remove cell phones, any computer accessible to them, and yourself, depriving them of an audience.

Sarcasm is a cloaked, cutting verbal attack described in the old proverb, "Sarcasm is the weapon of the weak man." It is so hurtful and humiliating that you must be very careful not to use it with your teenagers. In fact, it's best to eliminate it from your home entirely.

When you do hear sarcasm, you need to confront it because something else may be going on in your teen's mind that is being conveyed to you in this veiled way. You need to ask, "What is so wrong or is such a problem that you feel you have to be sarcastic with me?" Your goal is to redirect the conversation toward a positive end. Paul said, "Do not let any unwholesome talk come out of your mouths, but only what is helpful for building others up" (Eph. 4:29 NIV).

We all have a deep desire to be understood, even if there is not agreement. For your teens, just to know that you care enough to seek to understand their point of view can enable them to let go of enough of their anger to meet you halfway. This is what it will take to give your relationship depth. Otherwise all you have is a shallow existence with your kids, without any effective teaching or learning going on.

WHAT COULD YOU SAY?

During a confrontation with your teens about their language, you may want to say something like, "I realize you have issues with me, and I respect your right to form your own opinions. I want you to be able to share them with me. But in order for me to hear you, I need for you to express yourself in such a way that I *can* hear you. I have a hard time filtering out a hostile, sarcastic tone of voice in order to hear what's really on your mind and heart. Why don't you take a couple of deep breaths and let your anger dissipate a little, then we'll see if we can't talk this through. I need you to know that I'm serious enough about this issue to ground you from all activities and privileges until we can work it out. I love you, and I respect both of us too much to allow disrespectful, angry words to pass between us." Wise King Solomon said, "Words from a wise man's mouth are gracious, but a fool is consumed by his own lips" (Eccles. 10:12 NIV).

WISDOM FROM GOD'S WORD

Anger begets anger. That's why your challenge is this: don't let your angry teenagers spur you to respond in anger. Instead live out this practical truth, which your teen needs to learn to live out:

> A soft answer turns away wrath, but a harsh word stirs up anger. (Prov. 15:1)

Additional related resources (audio and print) are available from Hope for the Heart (http://www.hopefortheheart.org/):

Critical Spirit

6

Shirking Chores

"Kerry—come here, please! You agreed to clean off the table. No, you *can't* wait until after the TV show!" You feel anxious because the Mortons are arriving for dinner in less than thirty minutes.

"Julie, I asked you to pick up everything off the floor an hour ago. What have you been doing?" Although you're trying to talk to your teenagers, you feel like you're talking to the air.

"Tom—your deadline for getting the yard work done was *yesterday.* Absolutely *nothing* has been done!" You know your teenagers have been shirking their responsibilities. This is nothing new.

WHAT COULD YOU DO?

First, understand that you are not doing your teenagers a favor by allowing them to get by without helping at home. Galatians 6:5 says, "For each will have to bear his own load." Whenever they leave your home, whether it's to live with roommates or with a marriage partner, the idea that they are too "special" to do menial work will not make for a happy home in their new living situation.

For example, if your daughter cannot understand the obligation she has to her housemates to clean up after herself, she may suffer the repercussion of not having housemates for long. Then she may ask to come back home . . . just when you get used to seeing everything neat and orderly . . . possibly putting you in the unenviable position of having to practice tough love by saying no. One important point to emphasize to your daughter is that being faithful to do her chores is a way to show respect for those who are closest to her.

Early on, when America was an agricultural society, it was commonly understood that children would have significant chores around the house or farm. But with the lifestyle of the twenty-first century, many teenagers consider themselves too important to have household chores. (I recently saw a poster that seemed to express the mood of the day: "Teenagers: Tired of being hassled by your parents? Act now! Move out while you still know everything.")

The inescapable fact is, *everyone* in the home should share in the responsibilities that keep a household running smoothly. All who live at home have general responsibilities that include taking care of personal bedrooms by keeping them clean—making beds and picking up items from the floor.

Individual responsibilities are daily or weekly assignments, such as taking out the trash, cleaning the kitchen, mowing the lawn, vacuuming, sweeping the sidewalk, and doing the laundry. Some teenagers know exactly which chores are theirs, but they don't do them without constant reminders.

Once you decide on a fair allocation of chores, explain your rationale to your teenagers during a "family council meeting." Have them repeat to you what they've heard and present any scheduling problems.

After the problems are ironed out, everyone agrees, and that's it! Post the schedule. No grumbling allowed. Otherwise it becomes a never-ending argument. "Why do I have to do the dishes? I did them last night." "Why do I have to clean the windows? They're not dirty." "Why do I have to cut the grass? It's not that high."

If you have established who should complete each chore and by when—in writing—then you can hold your ground without resorting to the old parental groaner, "Because I said so." You can do this because increased responsibility is rewarded with increased freedom. This means you hold the trump card: your daughter's personal freedom depends on whether she has done her assigned chores *to your satisfaction*. That is, she cannot leave to spend time with her friends until her room passes inspection!

One mother offered this insight:

> My favorite phrase for dealing with messy rooms (or poor grades or a bad attitude) is: "That's not like you." It's a truism that children actually live up to, or down to, our expectations of them. If I see that Jennifer's room is trashed—again—and say, "You are such a slob!" that just reinforces her notion that she can't keep her room clean. She won't even try.

> The first time I used this tactic with Jennifer about her room, I remarked, "This clutter isn't like you. You're usually so well organized." She rolled her eyes and looked at me as if I were a bold-faced liar. She even said, "You're crazy! I'm not organized!" I said, "Maybe you haven't acted that way recently, but you're really an organized person on the inside."
>
> Seeing results from this has taken time because I had to change the way I speak to her, and she had to change her perception of herself. But it's paying off.

Now, about the laundry, don't let your teens' dirty clothes give you the "wash-day blues." Draw the "clothes line" and stay behind it: laundry that does not make it to the hamper does not get washed. If Kent really wants his favorite red shirt for Friday, he will somehow find the strength to move it ten feet from the floor to the hamper, but in no way will the designated laundry person be forced to search out his dirty clothes.

Do not take responsibility for making sure your teenagers do their chores. They may pretend not to understand, but you have already discussed these responsibilities and have put them in writing. They may choose to "forget," but you must choose not to nag.

If you give your teenagers the same instructions over and over again, you are teaching them that they don't have to obey until you've said it the fourth, fifth, or sixth time. You must discipline yourself to enforce the repercussions if the chores aren't done. This is the harder task because your teen will come up with the most heartrending excuses imaginable.

On a proactive note, plan time with your teens to invite them to share their ideas on reasonable responsibilities they can assume regarding the tasks that need to be done. Brainstorm how these could best be accomplished in light of their school and study schedules. Collaboration will help your teens take ownership of their roles . . . and be responsible to do their share of family chores. If they see this as *training for the future* when they are on their own, it further facilitates their desire to help.

WHAT COULD YOU SAY?

Let's say your son should have mowed the lawn by 6:00 PM Saturday. Now it's 6:45, and he's heading out the door. He says, "I promise I'll do it tomorrow. I give you my word. Susie finally agreed to go out with me, and I'll look like a total dork if I tell her I can't go because I have to mow the lawn. Please don't do this to me. Please! She'll never speak to me again."

With calm, sober sympathy, stretch out your hand for his car keys. "I'm so sorry, Kent. I want you to be able to go out with Susie, but it was your choice to sleep late this morning and watch sports this afternoon instead of mowing the lawn. You've known all week that you couldn't go anywhere today until that was done. Susie will forgive you."

If he misses his date, he will learn:

- You mean what you say.
- His obligation to keep his word to his parents takes precedence over his obligations to friends.
- He cannot alter agreements with you when it suits him.
- You are still in charge.

And I would venture to say that next week Kent will do his chores on time so he can be rewarded with the privilege of taking Susie out . . . and yes, Susie will still be speaking to him.

Remind your teens, "Being part of a family has rights and responsibilities. One of these responsibilities is service." The Bible says, "Through love, serve one another" (Gal. 5:13). Later, as an encouragement, you may say, "Soon you will be out on your own. Doing chores now is 'basic training' to prepare you for that time. In fact, you may even want to consider taking on more and more responsibilities so you will be even better prepared for when you have your own place."

WISDOM FROM GOD'S WORD

Since most teenagers are known for having bottomless pits when it comes to food, perhaps this Scripture will have a motivating impact.

> If anyone is not willing to work, let him not eat. (2 Thess. 3:10)

Additional related resources (audio and print) are available from Hope for the Heart (http://www.hopefortheheart.org/):

Procrastination

7

Driving Dangerously

It's Monday, and you're feeling it. So many things have gone wrong today that you can't imagine how it could get worse . . . until you get a phone call. "Uh, Dad? It's Lane. Uh, Dad, I need you to come pick me up at the corner of Mockingbird and Central. I had a little fender bender. I'm not hurt. It was just a really minor thing.

"No, I can't drive it. The right front fender's, like, crumpled around the tire. Police? Uh, huh . . . yeah, a ticket for speeding, and uh, following too closely. But, don't worry, I'll pay for it, no problem. Uh, Dad, by the way, I'm gonna need your car to pick up Lisa tonight."

There's no more volatile combination than teens and cars, but our largely suburban lifestyle makes mobility for teenagers almost a necessity for busy families. Be prepared when, as almost inevitably happens, your teen proves himself irresponsible with the family car.

WHAT COULD YOU DO?

One Chicago family's experience is instructive here. The mother writes:

> One day in the mail I discovered a letter from the secretary of state. It informed us that our teenager had received a speeding ticket, and if he receives just one more, there will be stiff legal penalties. Just a friendly note from the Illinois secretary of state! They must know that teenagers don't divulge that information. Our son certainly did not.
>
> I showed the letter to my husband, and we set our son down at the kitchen table for a lengthy talk. He admitted to getting the ticket five months ago. He had paid the fine secretly, hoping to avoid a parental confrontation. Of course, he did not realize that the fine was only part of the official consequences for his speeding.
>
> Other consequences came swiftly: We grounded him from using the car for a specified period of time. He also was grounded from certain

51

privileges for an even longer period of time. The biggest consequence, however, was the one he brought on himself by his ignorance of the law. Had he owned up to his mistake, we could have shown him the appropriate means to handle the ticket.

Notice the repercussions of doing it his way:

1. There was a $95 fine.
2. We lost his "Good Student Driver" discount on our car insurance. He now must pay the difference of $153.
3. The violation is now on his driving record (hence the discontinuation of the discount on insurance).
4. One more speeding ticket could lead to a two-year suspension of his driver's license.
5. The most drastic possibility is that his license could be revoked.
6. This hangs over his head for two years.

Notice the rewards of doing it under the parents' guidance:

1. He would have chosen to go to court, thus paying a lesser fine.
2. The violation would not have gone on his driving record.
3. The "Good Student Driver" discount would have remained in effect.
4. His license would not be suspended should he get another ticket.
5. The threat of a revoked license would not be quite as likely.
6. The "reprimand" period would be less than two years.

This lesson cost him over $200!

It stands to reason that whatever damage a teen driver causes to a vehicle, he pays the repair bill out of his own pocket (if he was at fault). The shock of discovering that replacing a bumper costs $800 to $1,200—conservatively—will make cautious drivers out of most cash-strapped teens. Proverbs 13:13 (NIV) says, "He who scorns instruction will pay for it, but he who respects a command is rewarded."

(Some parents have put a bumper sticker on their teen's vehicle that says, "How's my driving? Call [parent's phone number]." While this is excruciatingly embarrassing to teens, it can also be a deterrent to dangerous hotdoggers.)

WHAT COULD YOU SAY?

"Son, I'm deeply grateful to God for protecting you from injury. It sounds like you or someone else could have been seriously hurt, considering the damage done to your car. I'm grateful you will not have to live with the devastating repercussions if that had happened.

"I think God has given us both a wake-up call, and we need to heed His warning. Breaking the law and wrecking your car says to me that you need to take more responsibility for your actions and have more maturity under your belt before you get behind the wheel again. It will be a hardship on your mom and me to provide all of your transportation, but we will manage.

"The important thing is that you learn from this mistake. We'll talk later about how you're going to pay for your tickets and for repairs on the car and when you will attend a defensive driving course. I'm confident that you can become more responsible and regain our trust. Devise a plan and bring it to us within three days." Proverbs 9:9 says, "Give instruction to a wise man, and he will be still wiser; teach a righteous man, and he will increase in learning."

WISDOM FROM GOD'S WORD

Just as God's laws are boundaries to keep believers in line, civil laws are boundaries that keep all of us in line. Teens who cross over the line need to be on a correction course. Ultimately God's laws are safeguards for our lives.

> Submit yourselves to every human institution for the sake of the Lord. . . . For it is the will of God that by your good conduct you should put ignorance and stupidity to silence. (1 Pet. 2:13, 15 NEB)

8

Breaking Curfew

Danny is out on his first solo date. You know the girl and like her. You know where they're going and what they'll be doing. You've covered the ground rules thoroughly. But you're still a little uneasy.

You also know Danny's tendency to push against the boundaries. He doesn't think he *breaks* rules—he just *bends* them a little. His curfew tonight is 11:00 PM, but you're not confident that he'll take the time seriously. Sure enough, he walks in smiling and relaxed at 11:10. Your response to this is important.

WHAT COULD YOU DO?

Curfew is often the number-one conflict between parents and teens. Teens want to be out at night, and their parents want them in. In the case of a broken curfew, repercussions are called for because if Danny gets away with coming in a little late this time, he'll think nothing of coming in even later the next time. Still, you don't want to go ballistic over ten minutes.

When you're setting curfew with your teens, establish the repercussions down to the minute. That way there is no room for ambiguity or charges of unfairness. For instance, you might agree that for every ten minutes they come in past curfew, the next curfew will be shortened by twenty minutes (double the amount of time they were late). Secure their agreement before they leave, and yes, you need to synchronize watches!

Always being consistent when enforcing boundaries is imperative. Although ten minutes may not seem like a big deal, inconsistency sends the wrong message. As a parent, you will begin to lose credibility if you waiver. Matthew 5:37 (NIV) says, "Simply let your 'Yes' be 'Yes,' and your 'No,' 'No.'"

Hold your ground! Consistency and fairness with every decision is not only the right thing to do but is also a good role model for when they become parents. Again, have the courage to build self-discipline.

If they complain about your splitting hairs, emphasize that the reason for exactness is to make sure you are being fair. If they are as much as ten minutes late, they will know without being told that their curfew next time will be 10:40 PM. If they return home on time at the adjusted curfew, then you can reward them by reestablishing their original curfew of 11:00 PM

If your teens are developing a habit of breaking curfew, you will have to consider stronger measures, such as limiting their activities to events when they have you or another responsible person as a driver.

On the other hand, you could decide to eliminate the activities that give them the most trouble.

In all fairness though, you need to recognize that some activities, such as school athletics, at times run longer than expected. You might have to say something like, "I expect you to come home immediately after the football game." If they fail to do so, then they lose their privilege to go to the next football game.

Admittedly, on some occasions the issue of curfew becomes moot. For instance, theater or band rehearsals are notorious for lasting into the wee hours. If your teens wish to participate, they will simply need to come home immediately when the rehearsal is over. Of course, such late hours can be particularly difficult on parents who have to go to work early the next morning.

About the only thing you can do is become involved in the activity's booster club. Not only will you have an opportunity to observe the inner workings of the group, you will have a schedule for projected late nights. Since school districts have rules about how long directors can keep students on school nights, you need to be informed. Then you will have a better opportunity to know whether your teens are where they are supposed to be, doing what they are supposed to do.

WHAT COULD YOU SAY?

You could say something like, "I know you want to go out with your friends on your own, and I want that for you, too. But it is important for both of us to know that you can be trusted to keep your word. And that means coming home when you say you will. God's Word says, 'Whoever can be trusted with very little can also be trusted with much' (Luke 16:10 NIV). Honoring your curfew may seem small to you, but to me it's an indicator of your ability to be trusted with more responsibility and privileges.

"I need to know I can count on you to do what you say. If you're late, I'll start to worry, and if I'm worried, I'll start calling around to check up on you. I don't think you want me to call other parents at 2:00 in the morning!

"If getting home on time proves to be difficult for you, we'll shorten your curfew by twenty minutes for every ten minutes you are late. Then we'll return to your original curfew after you make the new curfew once. If you continue to come in late, I will have to go back to driving the car for you until you've developed the discipline of keeping your curfew. If you can think of a better way to make sure you get home on time, let me know, and we'll talk about it."

WISDOM FROM GOD'S WORD

One of the most trying lessons for teenagers has to do with time—how to be conscious of time when they're with friends who have no curfew. While time constraints can feel painful, in the long run they produce peace.

> No discipline seems pleasant at the time, but painful. Later on, however, it produces a harvest of righteousness and peace for those who have been trained by it. (Heb. 12:11 NIV)

9

Sneaking Out

Your fifteen-year-old daughter Amber has developed a crush on a nineteen-year-old high school dropout. You are adamantly opposed to her seeing him and have told her so. One Saturday she comes to ask permission to go to a party where you know she will see this boy. You refuse, and she runs to her room crying.

Hours later, in the middle of the night, you get up for a drink of water. Vague suspicions have crept into your mind; you go to your daughter's bedroom and quietly open the door. Amber's bed is empty. She is gone.

Some teens seem to have an urgent need to test boundaries, including physical boundaries. There is something almost irresistible and empowering about sneaking out after hours. Welcome to the ranks of parents with teenagers who won't stay put for the night!

WHAT COULD YOU DO?

A forty-year-old woman confided, "When I was seventeen, I often climbed out of my bedroom window at night to meet a married man. When my parents got wind of the fact that I was going out the window, my dad bolted the screen shut. Other than that, they never said a word to me. That didn't stop me, of course. I just started using the back door. But if we'd had a fire that blocked the hallway, I would have fried!"

She reflected, "I know what *would* have stopped me . . . if they had just confronted me. It really would have made a difference for them to say, 'We love you too much to let you destroy your life by doing this.' I would have respected that. I knew what I was doing was wrong, but I didn't have the moral backbone to stop. I needed their help." Bottom line, she wanted limits with love. She got the limits but not the love . . . so the limits didn't work.

Another woman who considered herself to have been a good teenager confided, "I didn't normally have a need to push the envelope and therefore had few restrictions. I was a lifeguard and loved to swim. I would sneak out of my room at night and drive out to a lake and go swimming all alone. Water was always very relaxing for me, and it gave me great time to think and reflect. It never once crossed my mind that I could be in danger or that if I drowned, no one would know where I was. I have thought back on this many times when considering the fact that teenagers often do not have the wisdom to see the cause and effect of their decisions."

Prohibition is not the only stance a caring parent can take. The choices are not just two—limits or liberty. You can be creatively proactive, especially if you see the signs of sneakiness lurking around the corner.

- Take your teens to observe the emergency room at the county hospital on a Friday or a Saturday night between 11:00 PM and 5:00 AM.
- Do computer research together, focusing on employment opportunities and criminal statistics for high school dropouts.
- Ride around in a police patrol car during the late shift on a weekend night.
- Research the statistics on violent crimes committed between dusk and dawn during weekends.
- Attend a community service program and a neighborhood watch program on violent crime protection.
- Check newspaper stories for incidents involving crimes committed at night against teens in your city. Consider meeting with one or more victims who will share their story with your teen.

In contrast, a Denver mom relates this experience:

One evening our fourteen-year-old daughter had two girlfriends staying overnight. At 2:00 in the morning, these girls decided to call a taxi to go over to a boy's house. A neighbor of ours called in a complaint of prowlers to the sheriff.

He came out to investigate while the taxi was still sitting in front of our house. The sheriff asked the taxi driver who he was waiting for, and he gave them our address and phone number. The sheriff called us to ask if we had requested a cab. I said no, but then I got suspicious.

In between the time the sheriff called and I got downstairs to check on the girls, they had sneaked out the back door, got into the taxi, and taken off. I called the sheriff's office. When they finally contacted the driver, he had already dropped off his fares at an intersection near downtown. I called both of the other girls' parents, and we all got in our cars to circle the intersection. The police were also out looking for them.

Around 4:00 AM one mom followed a taxi all the way back to our house, where 'guess who' got out. Their parents came for them immediately, and the next morning all the girls and parents met at our house.

My husband, an administrator of a Christian organization, proceeded to "investigate" the incident with clipboard in hand. As it turned out, the girls did go to this boy's house, a fourteen-year-old who had two other boys sleeping over. My husband, taking notes on his clipboard, grilled the girls individually about everything, including who was there, what they drank or ate, and who was wearing what.

The girls admitted they entered the boy's house through his bedroom window, watched a movie, ate snacks, drank soft drinks, and then left again through the bedroom window. My husband then called the three boys to our house and proceeded to "investigate" the matter with them as well. They were scared to death! He directed them to confess the incident to their parents and then call him confirming that they had done so within twenty-four hours. If they didn't follow through with these conditions, he would call the parents himself. All the boys complied.

The purposes in a man's heart is like deep water, but a man of understanding will draw it out (Prov. 20:5).

WHAT COULD YOU SAY?

Teenagers who sneak out of the house are not rare exceptions, but a healthy, mature confrontation with unconditional love is. You will be a hero in their hearts as you learn how to enforce limits with love.

You might say, "We know you're growing up and making more and more of your own decisions. One day you will be making all the decisions that affect your life, but as parents who love you, we still have the responsibility to guide you and discipline you for all inappropriate, dangerous, or harmful behavior.

"Sneaking out of your room at night and going somewhere we don't want you to go with someone we don't want you dating is totally unacceptable! We are hurt and disappointed that you would blatantly defy us like this. We knew you were upset that we didn't give you permission to go to the party, but we trusted you to honor our wishes. Until we are convinced that we can trust you in the future, you are grounded. If you continue to defy us, you will remain grounded. Sneak out again, and we will call the police. These are non-negotiable, not because we don't care about you, but because we *do* care about you." The Bible tells us, "For the moment all discipline seems painful rather than pleasant, but later it yields the peaceful fruit of righteousness to those who have been trained by it" (Heb. 12:11).

What happened in the case of the daughter from Denver? Her mother shares the rest of the story:

> As a repercussion, our daughter was grounded with no outside activities besides church for two months (she was gone for two hours). A good attitude was mandatory. After four weeks, we lifted her grounding as a reward for good behavior. She indicates now that the worst part of the whole thing was the investigation via clipboard. My husband's handling it in an official manner gave all the kids an appreciation for the seriousness of the matter, not just for their deception, but for putting themselves at risk by being out in a taxi in the middle of the night.

As with most issues that have escalated and have become more complex in today's culture, so has the issue of running away. The number of teens who have left home with no intention of returning is increasing. These are teens who have gone beyond the teenage prank behavior of sneaking out and have literally left home and family behind.

Some even feel justified, seeing no problems with meeting someone they have been communicating with on the Internet. Tragically, the potential risks and repercussions, such as sexual assault, trafficking, slavery, and kidnapping, have become more frequent and frightening.

The brain of a teenager lacks the maturation needed to develop wisdom and often cannot predict long-term repercussions for short-term actions. What may seem like a simple fun activity such as sneaking out, meeting someone, or running away for a night to "teach parents a lesson" can have painful consequences beyond their comprehension. For some, the reality check comes too late.

As your teens strive to earn their freedom, encourage them to give serious thought to those choices that could change the course of their lives forever. All choices have consequences, both good and bad, both rewards and repercussions. Again, the goal as parents is to help teens establish a good, inner moral compass that directs them away from any choices that could drastically and hurtfully change the course of their future or cause harm to themselves or to someone else.

WISDOM FROM GOD'S WORD

One of the things that causes the most concern about teenagers is their abundant lack of common sense when it comes to heading into harm's way. Discipline can be an effective deterrent—a safeguard for every teen.

> Discipline your son, for in that there is hope; do not be a willing party to his death. (Prov. 19:18 NIV)

10

Telephone Abuse

You're at home, expecting an important business call on your landline that should have come twenty minutes earlier. Out of concern you pick up the receiver—and hear your daughter's voice. You interrupt the conversation saying, "Holly, I'm so sorry, but I'm expecting a call. Will you please hang up the phone?"

"Sure, Mom," she chirps. So you hang up, but five minutes pass and the phone still does not ring. Tentatively you pick up the receiver and hear Holly's voice again.

"Holly! You said you were getting off the line!"

"Gee, Mom, keep your shirt on. I'm hanging up," she says. Once more you take her at her word, but five minutes later, with mounting suspicion, you check the line again, only to hear Holly's honeyed voice going strong. It's time for a new tactic.

WHAT COULD YOU DO?

Many families resolve the problem of teens' monopolizing the home phone by buying cell phones or separate telephone lines for them. But as often happens, if friends call on their line and can't reach them, they will call on their parents' line.

Teens are best served by learning courtesy and time management. Therefore it is often helpful to restrict use of the phone by insisting on:

- no calls during mealtime
- no calls during study time
- no calls after 10:00 PM
- no calls when an incoming call is expected by someone else
- no staying on the phone when someone else wants to use it
- no interruptive, operator-assisted emergency calls from their friends (unless it is a true emergency)

Failure to follow these guidelines results in suffering the repercussion of losing telephone privileges for a certain amount of time.

- If your teens share a phone line with anyone else, an automatic time limit—say, twenty minutes—should be set on all calls. If this is an ongoing rule, it can help preclude fights over having the phone tied up when someone else is expecting a call.
- Make it clear that your teens are expected to surrender the phone immediately for someone else's emergency (even if they do not consider the need urgent). They will have emergencies for which they will expect immediate use of the phone. This is a great opportunity for learning the practicality of the Golden Rule.
- Any unauthorized long-distance calls or any charges incurred for frills (such as three-way calling) will have to be paid by them.

WHAT COULD YOU SAY?

To keep your teenagers from monopolizing the telephone, explain, "I know you enjoy talking with your friends, and I want you to be able to talk with them, too. I also know you need to demonstrate respect for the rest of the family by keeping some rules for phone usage. Philippians 2:3 says, 'In humility count others more significant than yourselves.' Being mindful of the telephone needs of other family members is one way to do that. If you break the rules, your phone privileges will be totally revoked for the next two days. That's not what I want for you, but it's your choice whether privileges are revoked or not. My desire is that you will keep the rules and reap the reward of your having your privileges extended. I want you to be courteous and not continue a phone conversation when someone else in the family needs the phone. First Corinthians 13:4–5 (NLT) says, 'Love is not . . . rude. It does not demand its own way.'

"Of course, the number-one rule is that you not use the phone during family meals, homework time, or after bedtime. I will answer the phone at these set times and take messages for you. It is best that you tell your friends not to call during mealtimes, homework time, or after 10:00 PM. Also, during school nights you need to limit your phone conversations to twenty minutes.

"On weekends you can talk longer as long as you release the phone when someone else needs to use it. If someone calls while you are on the telephone, you will need to find out who it is and release the phone if the call is for your father or me. If the call is for someone else in our family, you will need to limit the rest of your call to five minutes. You can just take a message if the person being called is not here.

"Make it clear to your friends that under no circumstances are they to make an emergency phone call through the operator in an attempt to talk with you. There may be times when your father or I will ignore call waiting if we are on an important call and do not want to be interrupted. That is something you, on the other hand, are not allowed to do. There are just some privileges that go with paying the bill. I don't want you talking on the telephone all night and neglecting your family. We enjoy your company too much for that."

WISDOM FROM GOD'S WORD

Teaching your teenagers to treat others with respect in regard to the telephone is not only helpful—it also follows the Golden Rule:

> Whatever you wish that others would do to you, do also to them. (Matt. 7:12)

11

Cell Phone Abuse

At the end of your meeting, you turn your cell phone back on and discover the school has called three times and sent one text. It's the principal. Your teen has been called into the office for repeatedly using a cell phone in class.

Annoyed, you start to listen to the message while thinking, *How many times have I said, "Don't take your cell phone into class"*? The principal says you *must* come and pick up your teen. She has just been suspended!

Back in the "good ole days" telephones had a cord that kept teens on a "leash" and under control! Parents knew to whom their teens were talking and when. At best a teen could drag the cord around the corner or into a closet for privacy. As parents you decided to whom your teen could talk on the phone. But then is not now!

Here's the irony. The "ole days" may have kept teens physically close with the phone cord when they were home, but when they went out, parents had no way of knowing where they were. Cell phones offer parents a sense of security when teens are out and about because they can call and talk with them anytime, anywhere. This also means that when teens are at home in the presumed security of their own bedrooms, they can also call anyone, anywhere. And without boundaries on that phone, they can do much more.

Currently an area of serious concern is the ability of teens to send text messages to each other, even without appearing to do so. They can have the cell phone in a pocket and send messages and pictures to their friends while seeming to pay attention to something else, such as classwork . . . or you. According to Nielsen, American teens send and receive, on average, thousands of text messages a month.[1]

In many respects, teens and young people have created a language and subculture of their own—one most adults cannot even interpret. Pictures are also sent via the cell phone. Sending photos and messages of a sexual nature—called *sexting*—is also becoming alarmingly commonplace among teens, a practice that can be prosecuted as child pornography, a serious criminal offense.

Parents need to set boundaries about how this new technology will be used and reach agreements with their teenagers. A starting point could be a signed agreement detailing the boundaries, confirming your teens' acceptance and understanding.[2]

With no boundaries guiding cell phone usage, your teens can:

- access inappropriate television programs
- view movies with unsuitable ratings (lying about age to gain access)
- access music channels containing vulgar content
- spend excessive time gaming
- participate in peer-to-peer file sharing with a potential legal penalty
- use video chat rooms
- experience virtual sex and pornography of every kind

WHAT COULD YOU DO?

Wise parents monitor their teens' cell phone usage. Knowing that the cell phone can be inspected at any time may keep teens more accountable.

- Before giving your teen a cell phone, communicate the ground rules for its use.
- Request a detailed statement each month listing phone numbers in order to keep tabs on outgoing and incoming calls and messages.
- Limit the number of text messages your teens can send within a given time period.
- When a rule is ignored, implement repercussions.
  — Restrict their phone privileges for a reasonable period.
  — Communicate what, specifically, will be required to regain the lost privileges.
- Work with your wireless provider to implement parental controls.
- Limit the amount of time your teens can be on the phone to talk or text. Take the phone away during homework, during meals, and at bedtime.
- Lead by example. You don't have to take every call or read every incoming text immediately. If you are with others, converse in person.
- Model and train your teen in communication etiquette.

Follow Paul's wisdom to set "an example by doing what is good. In your teaching show integrity, seriousness and soundness of speech that cannot be condemned" (Titus 2:7–8 NIV).

WHAT COULD YOU SAY?

"While I don't like what you did, I will always love you. You abused the privilege of your cell phone, and now you have to earn it back. Right now let's take one thing at a time, beginning with your education." If your teen reacts in anger, remember that the anger is a secondary emotion, masking the real issue, which may be fear and embarrassment. Be patient. Emotions in teens are powerful. Teens focus on the now and are often unable to see tomorrow. Assure them, "This is now, and now is not forever."

"This is what I expect." Clearly define your rules for using a cell phone. Then tell them, "You will also need to submit a plan to me for how you intend to earn back your phone privileges. We'll move forward from there." It is imperative to deliver firm expectations along with unconditional love.

Look at the heart of this insightful Scripture: "The Lord disciplines those he loves, and he punishes everyone he accepts as a son. Endure hardship as discipline; God is treating you as sons. For what son is not disciplined by his father? . . . No discipline seems pleasant at the time, but painful" (Heb. 12:6–7, 11 NIV).

WISDOM FROM GOD'S WORD

Show me your ways, O LORD, teach me your paths; guide me in your truth and teach me, for you are God my Savior, and my hope is in you all day long. (Ps. 25:4–5 NIV)

12

Objectionable Music

Your arms loaded with grocery sacks, you nudge the door to your house open with your foot, only to be blasted backward by a high volume of heavy-metal guitar riffs. The walls are shaking, and dishes are vibrating. "Matt!" you shout, trying to be heard. "MATTHEW!" It's hopeless. Matt doesn't even realize your presence until—hands over your ears—you make your way to the stereo and turn off the blaring sound. Matt looks up from the couch in surprise as you close your eyes in relief. Then, straining to maintain your composure, you calmly ask, "What are you listening to?"

Generational differences are never more apparent than in the music each prefers and the volume at which it is played. One mother shared, "I recently looked through the journal I keep about Clint and came across the following prayer he prayed a couple years ago. . . . 'Lord, help me—even when I get to be a teenager and I'm a juvenile delinquent—still to have a good relationship with my parents, so I won't turn into one of those people who listen to really loud music and ruin their hearing.' So far the Lord has answered this prayer. His tastes lean toward country music, and he doesn't like it loud. It seems his hearing is safe for the time being."

This boy is not typical. Today's teenagers seem to like screeching guitars and grating vocals or thumping bass beats and rhythmic riffs. In whatever genre, they like it LOUD because it feeds the emotional part of the brain as discussed in chapter 3. It's one thing to ask them to turn the volume down, which they will do if they want the privilege of listening to it at all. But what if the lyrics themselves are downright objectionable?

WHAT COULD YOU DO?

Teens simply love music. Exposing them to variety is the key. Establishing boundaries on what is acceptable in terms of the message is essential.

- Encourage them to think about what they are listening to. Play different kinds of music, and encourage them to talk about how each makes them feel.
- Help them discover music that uplifts the spirit and intellect rather than simply engaging the emotions. Praise music, hymns, and certain classical repertoires are good examples.
- Expose them to music with increasing depth. When they listen only to loud contemporary music, whether it's secular or Christian, often their ears can't discern the message. As a result, they react only to the beat, a purely emotional response. In the case of lyrics that promote a sexual, violent agenda, the words go into the subconscious and the teen isn't aware that the brain has registered them.
- Share music that was popular when you were growing up and have a good laugh about how concerned your parents were with your musical choices.

Today's technology further complicates your ability to influence your young person's musical choices. Teens often download music from the Internet to their digital music players and listen to it privately through headphones. As parents you often have no idea what they are listening to at any given time. But you *need* to know! Periodically ask your teens for their earphones and listen. Just do it respectfully.

As a parent, you are the gatekeeper. While each past generation has complained about the current generation's music, no one can debate the fact that much of the music today has gone to new depths of decadence. It degrades women as sex objects, disrespects those in authority, defames God and country, and deliberately advocates an agenda of violence.

Music is powerful because it goes straight to the emotion center of the brain. Even with just a few bars played, the music and message often continue to replay in the subconscious.

Certain music triggers a sexual response within the body. Today's music videos often portray visual images that are sexual and violent. The minds of teens are inundated with messages that hook them emotionally and paint graphic pictures that will be imbedded in their memory for years.

Listening to music generates chemicals in the brain called endorphins that can produce a response similar to a drug high. The teen brain is developmentally at a stage where it operates more from emotions and less from logic. Certain music feeds that need for excitement. Likewise, music has power to uplift us—as is the case with many classical pieces, hymns of the faith, and praise music.

- Don't react out of ignorance. Listen closely to the words of the music your teen is listening to. If the words are not discernible, access the lyrics on the Internet. Many teens today do not own actual music CDs. Have your teen read the song lyrics to you. Often teens are responding to the beat and do not pay close attention to all the words. Read the inserts of every music CD your teen purchases, and watch the music videos of those artists. Second Corinthians 10:5 says we are to "destroy arguments and every lofty opinion raised against the knowledge of God, and take every thought captive to obey Christ."
- Offer your teens alternatives. An explosion in the variety of Christian music has attracted teens by the thousands—contemporary music styles with lyrics that could be straight from the Psalms. Help them explore these options to find a sound they like with a message you like. If they resell or trade the objectionable CDs, you might offer to pay for one or two Christian CDs to start their new collection. (One warning: should the objectionable CDs be spiritually oppressive, consider destroying them.)
- Make an arrangement with your teens: for every two hours spent listening to their choice of music, they will listen to one hour of music you choose—music such as classical, hymns, jazz, or something unamplified to begin to stretch their musical taste.
- Be aware that even after you have put all these safeguards in place, your teens will still be able to access or download for free almost any music through computer software. While the wrangling goes on over the legality of music-sharing software, these programs are popular and readily available. Talk to your teens about music piracy and the rights of artists to earn a living from their music. Set a good example by refusing to obtain music illegally yourself.

WHAT COULD YOU SAY?

As in any conflict in which you are trying to find common ground, lead in love. Set a time to listen to music together. Ask them to bring some music they like. Play it for a few minutes. In a nonjudgmental way, ask them what they find appealing about it. Ask, "What kind of music do you think I listened to when I was a teen?" Let them guess and then name a few groups. They may be surprised . . . or genuinely shocked. The teachable moment is there—the door is open, and you can gently walk through it. Don't just preach about the "evils of music"—connect . . . listen . . . talk . . . share this time with your teen.

Pray for the right moment to say, "Music is powerful. It can influence body, soul, and spirit. Like a drug, it can alter your mind and mood. The Bible tells us, 'For as he thinks within himself, so he is' (Prov. 23:7 NASB). Although we won't always like the same things, I will always love you. But I can't find anything to like in this music. What do you think they mean by this?" Show your teen specifically what you object to and wait for a response (which will probably be noncommittal).

"I am sincerely concerned that you listen to messages like this and fill your mind with these kinds of thoughts. Your mind is like any other container—what goes in is what comes out. God designed you to fill your mind with pure and righteous thoughts so your words and actions honor Him. Put yourself in my shoes for a minute. Would you want your children singing words like these?

"Ultimately it's your decision as to what you choose to fill your mind. Because I love you, I want to encourage you to keep your mind pure, regardless of what everyone else is doing. Inevitably, what you listen to will shape your attitude, and your attitude will shape your actions. I want you to stay clear of the traps of a bad attitude because eventually that bad attitude will only hurt you.

"I also do not want to subject anyone else in this house to words like these. Therefore, this music is not to be played and needs to be discarded from your music collection. I also want to offer to purchase for you some music we both can feel good about, to replace what you've discarded. I have confidence that you will respect this decision and recognize that it is right in God's sight."

Establishing both the repercussions for violating your boundary and the rewards for keeping it can provide both the deterrent and the incentive needed to lead your teen to make a wise decision.

WISDOM FROM GOD'S WORD

The apostle Paul's counsel is practical and pertinent for today's teenage culture. He helps us know what to let into our minds, which then ultimately guards our hearts.

> Whatever is true, whatever is honorable, whatever is just, whatever is pure, whatever is lovely, whatever is commendable, if there is any

excellence, if there is anything worthy of praise, think about these things. (Phil. 4:8)

Additional related resources (audio and print) are available from Hope for the Heart (http://www.hopefortheheart.org/):

Satan, Demons, & Satanism

13

Media Mania

You walk into the family room while Trevor, your teenager, is watching a popular, prime-time comedy show. You're not really paying attention until a person on the show utters one of the most obscene remarks you've ever heard, and the room fills with canned laughter.

You've reached your limit. You're sick of the sexual sewage spewing out over the airwaves and on posters—all going directly into Trevor's brain. Obscenity, disrespect, and irreverence have become so pervasive in today's entertainment that it sometimes seems the only way to get away from it all is to find an uninhabited island on which to raise your teens. But what if you can't find your own island retreat?

The task of establishing boundaries in the area of media may seem like climbing Mt. Everest, a daunting task at best. Each past generation has had something to monitor in the younger generation, but it was manageable. Fast-forward to today and the list seems endless. A parent could play "media monitor" full-time and still miss something. The concerns are numerous:

- programs on television and cable networks
- movies with standards deliberately lowered in order to achieve ratings that attract wider audiences
- music: CDs, MP3 players, and iPods
- music videos spewing out sex, violence, and profanity
- video games with the goal to kill and destroy the opponent through various violent activities
- concerts with music that degrades women and upholds violence
- radio programs with DJs and hosts who consistently challenge the listeners' sense of decency
- magazines and books for teens that freely talk about sex, condone homosexuality, and infiltrate belief systems with compromising material

- simple webcams that enable teens to make personal "movies" and share among friends
- computer Web sites, chat rooms, and text messaging

Brain scans show that TV violence activates the amygdala, which aids in regulating responses of anger. Ramped-up aggression hormone production in teens corresponds to indulging in violent video game scenarios.[1]

Another problem on the rise for adolescents is video game addiction. Video game addicts exhibit all the same tendencies as people who are addicted to drugs or gambling.

WHAT COULD YOU DO?

It may be impossible for you as a parent to put enough boundaries in place to protect your teenagers from the bombardment of the entertainment industry. In a wireless world that has infiltrated the lives of our teens, it is imperative that you use great discernment when setting boundaries. Utilize:

- Prayer power
  — Pray for God's protection for your teens.
  — Prioritize time to pray *with* your teens.
  — Plan opportunities to study God's Word together.
- Proactive participation
  — Be available.
  — Be authentic.
  — Refrain from having the attitude of a spy—your goal is not to say "Gotcha" but rather to guide and protect. Communicate to your teens up front that you will be monitoring all media devices and will not sneak around to do so. See where your teens are going on the Internet, who they are texting, and what they are watching and reading. Establish firm guidelines, and be sure to have all their passwords—accountability encourages transparency, which helps build trust. This Sherlock Holmes attitude says, "I love you, and I'm here for you. I'm your safety net."
- Preventative precautions
  — Use teachable moments. If you're watching a football game and don't want your teens to see immodest cheerleaders, switch to another program at those times or, if you record the program, use the fast-forward button. Talk with your teens about why you choose to refuse allowing those visual images in your home.
  — Persevere because nothing is more important than the heart, mind, and soul of your teens.

The problem may be not that your teens are abusing media but spending every waking moment either on the computer, in front of the TV, or with earphones attached to their heads. One mother who became concerned about her son's electronic IVs (in this case, ideas or images ingested directly into the brain!) finally declared two hours every school night to be under an "electronic blackout." Any media device that required electricity or batteries was turned off during those two hours. Her son fought this restriction energetically for a while, but his grades in English improved noticeably.

Proverbs 19:20 (NIV) says, "Listen to advice and accept instruction, and in the end you will be wise."

WHAT COULD YOU SAY?

"I realize you are being bombarded on every side by media. The enemy wants to use it to deceive and entrap you to destroy you morally and physically. I understand some of what's going on, and I'm learning more. I always want to do what is best for you. This is a war we need to fight together. It would not be fair for me to leave you in this battle alone. I love you too much to leave you unprotected. From this day forward I will monitor the media outlets you use. I need you to link arms with me on this. Can I count on you?"

Communicate:

- "No topic is off-limits for you to bring to me with your concerns."
- "Let's talk about what we can do, especially in those areas where you feel most vulnerable."
- "What do you think we should do first? How can I most help you?"
- "What can you do to help maintain media boundaries for our home?"

"If you choose to make media choices that are not within the boundaries we have agreed upon, I will need to restrict your use of the computer (or music, television, phone, etc.). Likewise, if I see you making wise choices, I will not need to monitor you as often. Remember, my monitoring is only because I *do* love you and because I want to see if you can be trustworthy. In this world some pretty ugly things can sneak in without your even realizing it. I am always here to discuss any topic of your choice or to answer any questions about information to which you may be exposed."

Ecclesiastes 9:17 (NIV) says, "The quiet words of the wise are more to be heeded than the shouts of a ruler of fools."

WISDOM FROM GOD'S WORD

Teenagers' minds need to be challenged to move away from worldly thoughts and worldly things. Teens need to know that God can free anyone trapped in this Worldwide Web by totally transforming their minds.

> Do not conform any longer to the pattern of this world, but be transformed by the renewing of your mind. Then you will be able to test and approve what God's will is—his good, pleasing and perfect will. (Rom. 12:2 NIV)

14

Internet Hazards

You're running late for a meeting, and you've already packed your laptop when you realize you need to look for directions on the Internet. Your teen is at school, and you decide to use his computer. You have a ground rule that you can know the passwords, so you click away. The images that pop up leave you stunned and revolted.

You click again, and again, and again. With your heart in your throat your blood pressure quite possibly in a danger zone, you go on to check the laptop's browser history. You are numbed by the mere existence of the content you have just witnessed.

Retrieving the map, you unplug the laptop and put it in your car. As you drive, you pray and ponder, thoroughly perplexed. *He's a good kid, makes decent grades, goes to church without any arguments, complies with what I ask. Where in the world did this come from, and how long has it been going on?*

The new frontier is cyberspace, and it has come right into your home! The benefits are many, but the dangers are disastrous.

Probably the number-one threat of the Internet is the proliferation of easily accessible, hard-core pornography. The number of teens addicted to Internet pornography has exploded in recent years. Software programs that supposedly block dangerous sites are continually circumvented by ingenious pornographers. Your teen's innocent word searches can bring up tantalizing screens with veiled invitations that beckon like sirens: "The following HOT HOT HOT pix are for ADULTS ONLY. So don't click 'continue' unless you're over 18!" Be aware of the bait for sexually curious teens. Be *aware*, be *alert*, be *alarmed*.

THE INTERNET

Internet chat rooms offer visitors a place to meet and socialize. However, for impressionable teens the venue can be devastating . . . or even deadly. Besides the lure of virtual sex, the other dangerous aspect of chat rooms is the highly publicized use that pedophiles or sexual predators make of them to lure teens into in-person meetings, usually in private settings. Molestation or rape is not the worst that can happen here. Newspapers have carried graphic accounts of sex trafficking and murders stemming from online meetings. (See chapter 42 of this book, "Sexual Activity.")

Through online access, your teens can:

- have a social network of friends unknown to you
- e-mail or IM (instant message) anyone, anywhere, anytime
- write and read blogs
- keep an online journal
- post photos
- access pornography of any kind
- order harmful, even illegal items
- view objectionable programs on video-sharing Web sites and other sites

The majority of parents are not aware of how to monitor their children's Internet activity. They may feel they are too busy with work and other activities to check on their teens' electronic usage. They also may not fully realize the dire consequences of a teen's unrestricted Internet access . . . or how innocently their children can become entrapped. It's critically important to stay informed and *make* the time to monitor your teen's electronic activity.

WHAT COULD YOU DO?

Sit down with your teenager. If you are a single mom, consider informing your child's father of your discovery or call on a Christian of the same sex as your teen—one whom your child respects. Briefly explain that you discovered the objectionable content, and you need to discuss it together. Stay calm. If you blow up, your teen will do the same. In fact, he may anyway. It's easier to show anger than embarrassment, especially for a boy.

Warn your teens of the seductive and addictive power of porn. If your child doesn't know the story of Ted Bundy, watch Dr. James Dobson's interview with the serial killer (available on the Internet) just prior to his execution. Discuss it together. Agree on a proactive plan for how you can help your teen and hold him or her accountable for implementation.

Make your home safe from Internet misuse. Here's how to accomplish that:

1. Put all computers in an open, family area.
2. Establish a family policy that gives you access to address books, social networks, and all electronic passwords for frequent monitoring. Add yourself to your teens' "friends" list on social networking sites so you can interact with them and observe their interactions with others. Refusals will result in no computer access.
3. Install a Web filter, enable parental controls on your browser, or take advantage of a service that will track and generate a log of your teen's online activity.
4. Set limits on Internet usage.
5. Make a rule that no personal or family contact information is ever to be given out on the Web and *no* passwords shared, even with a friend. Explain why doing so is unsafe. Remember that teens live in the present, normally make emotional decisions, love feeling connected, and aren't good at foreseeing repercussions for their actions. Their compliance with this important point is your best preventative measure.
6. Give guidelines for what kinds of games can be played. Explain *why* games and music with unacceptable messages will not be tolerated in your home. Pray that this conversation will plant seeds for good decision making in the future.
7. Explain the legal ramifications of plagiarism and copying legally protected music files.
8. Stay connected with your teens so they feel comfortable coming to you when issues come up (and they will).
9. Educate yourself on all the technology your teen uses on a daily basis. Learn basic Internet navigation techniques. Again, the goal is safety.
10. Use the "Safe Use Agreement" form published by the National Coalition for the Protection of Children and Families, or make up your own form.[1] Have all computer users sign the agreement.
11. Take a look at any laptop or memory stick brought into your home, and make sure you drop by regularly to monitor usage. You have a right to determine what comes into your home. Again, be prayerful—you don't want to project a spirit of legalism or distrust.
12. View their Internet browser histories periodically, check e-mails for unrecognized names, and look at social network communication history and "friends" lists. Follow your teens' computer tracks.

WHAT COULD YOU SAY?

"I took your computer today because I used it to print out a map and was quite surprised and very disappointed to find inappropriate sites you've been visiting. I want the very best for you, and these sites are not what you need to be looking at, and we both know it.

"I'm not trying to restrict your activities unreasonably or to be a dictator. Your mind is very impressionable and imprints visual images. It absorbs and stores everything it sees and hears. The Bible says we are 'transformed by the renewal of our minds.' Conversely, we are deformed by the corrupting of our minds. This is why we need to closely guard and protect our minds from anything ungodly. God's Word tells us to 'Flee from youthful lusts and pursue righteousness, faith, love and peace, with those who call on the Lord from a pure heart' (2 Tim. 2:22 NASB). If we try to compromise with evil—or try to participate 'just a little,' we lose. God says there's only one way to handle lustful temptation, and that is to 'flee.' I want you to use and enjoy the computer as well as other means of entertainment, but with accountability.

"If you make unwise choices in how you use this computer, the repercussion will be the loss of its use except for school and work . . . and I will monitor it daily. Likewise, when you can demonstrate to me that you are making good decisions on how to use the computer, your privileges will be restored and even extended.

"I will be checking on a regular basis because pornography is extremely addictive. I want you to be a person of integrity. I am available to talk with you at any time about anything. If this is not something you feel comfortable talking with me about, I will find someone else equipped to help you. We'll get through this together."

Pray with your teens. Ask God to put a hedge of protection over their minds and to guard their eyes from looking at things that would be harmful.

WISDOM FROM GOD'S WORD

As with everything God has created for good, the Enemy has corrupted the Internet for evil. "Satan disguises himself as an angel of light" (2 Cor. 11:14).

As people who are fallen, we are naturally selfish. It is, therefore, easy to fall into the patterns of the world.

> I know that nothing good dwells in me, that is, in my flesh. For I have the desire to do what is right, but not the ability to carry it out. For I do not do the good I want, but the evil I do not want is what I keep on doing. Now if I do what I do not want, it is no longer I who do it, but sin that dwells within me. (Rom. 7:18–20)

SECTION III

Boundaries at School

During the academic year, a teenager involved in school-sponsored extra-curricular activities will spend more waking hours at school than anywhere else, including home. Therefore, problems arising from your teen's behavior will often be apparent at school first.

When you are not present to enforce the rules, what do you do when the boundaries are broken? Don't assume you are powerless as a parent. Even from home, you can set boundaries for school. The best boundary of all is for your student to see that you and the school are working together as a partnership!

15

Tardiness

The phone rings. You answer. The vice principal from your daughter's school informs you that Becky is habitually tardy to class. The reason seems to be that she's using the time between classes to socialize in the halls instead of getting to class. Because Becky doesn't have any classes with some of her closest friends, the only time she can talk to them at school is between classes. While you empathize with your daughter's desire to be sociable, Becky's habitual lateness is affecting her grades.

WHAT COULD YOU DO?

The first and best recourse for you as a parent facing this problem is to be more involved at your daughter's school. Get to know your teen's teachers, especially the one whose class time she's missing. Talking to the teacher firsthand (and not hearing your teen's version only) will help you understand the situation better, and it will also reassure the teacher of your concern and your support for him or her as your teen's teacher.

A vice principal at a middle school once told me, "Even if you disagree with some of the teacher's decisions, it's essential for you to maintain an attitude of respect, just as teachers have to treat parents they disagree with respectfully." If your teenagers hear you criticizing coaches, teachers, or administrators, they will lose respect for the school's authority. If you bad-mouth the school at night, it torpedoes those who are in charge of your teens during the day. Then they don't have a chance of getting your teens to cooperate.

The reverse is also true. A good rule is, "Support in public, confront in private." Be careful not to berate your teens in front of teachers or anyone else. Too many adults have mental tapes from childhood of their parents' saying in the presence of others, "You're so lazy! You're so slow! Why can't you do anything right?" Years later, even when they are established and successful adults, those tapes can play over and over again, curtailing their confidence. Therefore, confront both your teens and school authorities in private without the other being present—at least initially.

Once you discern that your teens are indeed guilty of socializing instead of getting to class on time, set appropriate boundaries for the situation. In other words, make sure the punishment fits the crime. Don't overreact. Conversely, don't refuse to act. In the case of tardiness, you might choose to add up all the times your teen missed from class—perhaps thirty minutes—then double the amount and add it to homework time. Each minute they're late to class adds another two minutes to homework time.

Another possibility is for the teens to make up the missed time in study hall. Some schools have policies in place whereby a certain number of tardies automatically draws a detention. Saturday detentions are especially effective.

Let's assume your teen experiences the repercussion of crossing the line—going to detention—but continues to be tardy for class. In that case you must elevate the repercussion until you reach a level that evokes a response. Since most teens are social critters, you could reduce the amount of time they socialize with friends after school and in the evenings. Set the restricted time at minutes of class missed squared (and they get a free algebra lesson as well)!

Realize that if you lecture without listening, you will be ineffective. Your teens must understand that you are on their side. If you set limits without love, you create alienation. They will want to get as far away from you as possible: "I can't wait until I'm eighteen and out of here!" Alienating your teens will not persuade them to accept your values. Lead your teenagers with love.

There may be legitimate reasons why your teens are continually tardy. In a large high school, a student might have third-period class on the south side of the first floor and fourth-period class on the north side of the second floor. Getting from one class to the other within the time allotted may be nearly impossible.

The class period following gym also may be difficult to make on time if the coach does not allow sufficient time for dressing.

Some teachers (being human) have a bad habit of keeping their students after the bell signals the end of class.

If any of these scenarios apply, it is even more imperative that you schedule a parent-teacher conference to help straighten out the matter. This is a golden opportunity to be a hero to your teens, which may greatly improve their cooperation with you in other areas.

Proverbs 16:21 (NIV) says, "The wise in heart are called discerning, and pleasant words promote instruction."

WHAT COULD YOU SAY?

Since we are told to speak the truth in love, how you communicate consequences to undisciplined teenagers is as important as the consequences themselves.

You might say, "Becky, I know spending time with your friends is very important to you. And I want you to know that it's important to me, too. But it's also important to both of us that you fulfill your responsibilities at school in order to prepare for your future. Since it's your responsibility to be on time for your classes and to spend the entire period in class, you owe yourself the schooling you've missed by being late.

"Because you know the school's rules about tardiness, yet still walk in late, you forfeit the right to decide how you're going to spend a certain amount of your free time. For one week all phone calls to and from friends are suspended. Your teachers have been notified to call me if you continue to be tardy. If you are not, you can earn back the phone privileges. If you are, we'll have to extend the restriction an extra two weeks, which I really don't want to do. It's up to you, honey.

"If you think there's something else we can do to resolve this, I'm willing to listen and do whatever it takes for you to regain control of your time."

All of us can heed these words from Job: "I waited for your words, I listened for your wise sayings, while you searched out what to say" (Job 32:11).

WISDOM FROM GOD'S WORD

Your teenagers are not the first teens to be tardy to class. By seeking counsel from school authorities you are being both wise and biblical.

Without counsel plans fail, but with many advisers they succeed. (Prov. 15:22)

Additional related resources (audio and print) are available from Hope for the Heart (http://www.hopefortheheart.org/):

Habits; Procrastination

16

Disrupting Class

You receive a call from the assistant principal stating that your seventeen-year-old son is being excessively disruptive in class. He's persistently talking . . . passing notes . . . poking fun . . . determined to cause laughter during class. In short, Josh refuses to focus on his role as a student. As a result, he is not only failing to learn but also making it difficult for others to learn. His teachers feel increasingly frustrated.

I'll never forget leading a Parents of Teens Workshop in which one parent described one of the most creative approaches to establishing a boundary with repercussions and rewards that I've ever heard. She shared how she handled her high school junior after the school called her at work to report his disruptive behavior.

That evening she asked, "How was school today?"

"Okay," he mumbled.

"Well, Josh, apparently it wasn't okay. I received a call from the school about your disruptive behavior, and they said it must change."

After asking him several questions (with unsatisfactory results), she said, "Son, I really want to help you. I've seen you exercise self-control in my presence. So I've decided that you must need me to go to school *with* you."

"No, Mom, I don't need that."

"Oh, yes," she responded pleasantly. "Actually I'm going to school with you tomorrow."

"Mom, you can't do that!" he objected.

"Well, I've already cleared it with the school. In fact, I'm going to sit beside you in every class."

"Mom . . . please . . . no!!!"

"Son, I love you too much to do nothing. So . . . I've already canceled all my clients for tomorrow. Josh, nothing you say will deter me—end of discussion."

Now think about it: at school the last thing a six-foot-tall seventeen-year-old wants is Mama walking with him every single place, sitting beside him in every class. But the next day that's exactly what happened and, I might add, with no disrupting behavior on his part.

When they returned home, she complimented his behavior and then asked, "Since today you displayed self-discipline, do you think you need me at school tomorrow?"

Of course, she already knew the answer. "No way!"

"Wonderful! If in the future you need me to help you be more disciplined," she said half-seriously, "I'll let the law firm know that I'll be with you at school instead of at work."

They gave each other a knowing look, and he knew she meant it!

Just listening to this wise mother enforce a repercussion impressed us all. Still, I needed to ask the follow-up question: "Did you ever hear from the school again?"

She paused, then smiled. "Not a peep!"

WHAT COULD YOU DO?

If this scenario seems to hit home—your home, that is—and if you have not previously established a boundary along with repercussions and rewards, you need to sit down with your teens to communicate what has been shared with you and get their side of the story.

Only the most "saintly" teens would not put a little spin on the situation to reflect more positively on themselves. Hopefully your teens will level with you. If they take ownership of their disruptive behavior and admit what they did wrong, it will be their responsibility alone to change the behavior. Explain that if it happens again, there obviously needs to be a repercussion to help them in class. For example:

- You will help by joining them in that particular class . . . or for multiple classes. Let them know you will give them the opportunity to correct their behavior on their own before you contact the teacher about visiting the class. However, if the disruption continues, you need to follow through by contacting the teacher or the principal to arrange to sit in on the class. Realize, if you go with your teen, it's imperative that you *not* become the focus of the class!
- If your schedule doesn't allow you to join your teen in school, you may want to find another respected adult relative to sit in for you. Even though this person is a relative, again you would first need to receive permission from the school.
- You may choose to set a different repercussion such as taking away social time with friends, just as your teens took away time in the classroom.

WHAT COULD YOU SAY?

Ask specifically what happened: "Is it true that you were disruptive in class? What did you do? [Wait for a response.] What were you supposed to be doing? [Wait for a response.] What are you going to do about it? [Wait for a response.]" Listen carefully, and refuse to go any further until you receive answers to those questions.

You might say, "Josh, I appreciate how entertaining you are, and I know how much fun it is to make the other kids laugh. Ecclesiastes 3:1 (NLT) says, 'For everything there is a season, a time for every activity under heaven.' And that includes clowning around.

"It's important you understand how frustrated your teacher feels when trying to compete with you for the class's attention. Remember how upset you were when your sister started talking over you at dinner? Well, the teacher has a certain amount of material she's required to cover each day, and when you're talking, she can't do that.

"You're mature enough to know when it's okay to joke around with your friends and when it's not. I know that you know what appropriate classroom behavior is, and I believe you have the self-control needed— you're just not exercising it. So . . . because you can exercise self-control around me, it seems you need my presence to remind you to stay quiet and to pay attention."

If your teens maintain that the teacher has an unwarranted grudge against them, you could counter, "It may be that the teacher is all wrong and you're right when you say you're not doing anything disruptive. But there has to be a reason she continues to be concerned about your behavior. The only way for me to find out what's really going on is to sit in on your class. When we both decide that you don't need me there any longer, I'll leave. The Bible says, 'Whatever happens, conduct yourselves in a manner worthy of the gospel of Christ. Then, whether I come and see you or only hear about you in my absence, I will know that you stand firm' (Phil. 1:27 NIV). I have every confidence that with the right motivation, you can exercise self-control in any situation. And I'm going to do whatever's necessary to help you do that, even if it's inconvenient for me and embarrassing to you." You'll be amazed at the effectiveness of this repercussion, and the reward will be great . . . for you both!

WISDOM FROM GOD'S WORD

By helping your children (of any age) check their disruptive chatter and tame their tongues, you enable them to develop more and more self-control and live their lives in line with the Bible. Since certain actions should be avoided, hand your kids this Scripture on an index card and encourage them to memorize it:

> Avoid godless chatter, because those who indulge in it will become more and more ungodly. (2 Tim. 2:16 NIV)

17

Cutting Classes

You are at work, up to your ears in deadlines, when the secretary at your daughter's school calls. Bethany's third-period teacher reported her absent. "Is she home sick today?" Your heart drops six inches. You know she left for school this morning. You mumble a hasty answer, "Thank you, I'll check into it," and disconnect to call home. The phone rings. The answering machine comes on. She's not at school, and she's not at home.

When students attain a certain level of confidence at their school, many will try to "beat the system" by cutting classes—that is, being absent from one or more classes without an approved excuse or a note from a parent. The problem is, not only are they missing necessary class instruction, but of greater concern, they are being deceptive. Such conduct clearly requires the setting of boundaries with relevant repercussions and rewards.

If a student is missing from school when overall attendance is taken and the school does not have a note or phone call from the parent, many times the school will call. If the parent is not aware of the teen's absence, the student is declared "truant" for the day, and someone may be sent to look for the student.

Truancy is defined as the unexcused, voluntary absence of a student from school for a set number of days per term. In certain cities, if your teen is truant for ten days or more in any six-month period, both you and your teen will be summoned before a family court judge to explain the reason for the absences. Since you don't want to find yourself in this predicament, you will want to be aware of your teen's attendance record. If the school is not efficient about calling you when your teenager skips, the first you may know of it is when you see a number other than zero in the "unexcused absences" column of your teen's report card. Once you discover the problem, you must act on it immediately.

WHAT COULD YOU DO?

Obviously, your first course of action is to talk to the prime suspect—your teenager—as soon as both of you get home. She may have all kinds of excuses, like, "The teacher wasn't paying attention. She never notices me. I was there." Answering this is easy: you call the teacher.

If the teacher confirms the absence, you may want to do a little probing by asking her these questions:

- Were any other students absent?
- Is my daughter having trouble in the class?
- Has she had other absences?
- Is she a discipline problem?

Although these questions may be difficult to ask, you need to hear whatever the teacher has to say.

Call the vice principal, the school counselor, and/or any police officer assigned to full-time duty at the school. Inquire as to whether they have noticed any changes in your teen of which you need to be aware. Although school officials are unable to disclose the names of other students, they may take the opportunity to let you know that they have noticed your teen hanging out with some new friends.

At that point it will be your responsibility to find out who the *new* friends are. Use your time with school officials to learn all you can about their perception of your teen at school. Keep the conference focused on your son or daughter.

Even if this incident of skipping school is not a pattern but only a one-time occurrence, find out why she skipped school and with whom. Talk with your teen about the situation. Listen with a calm, discerning spirit to what your teen has to say so you can gain a better understanding of the situation. Verbalize the boundary, and write out the repercussions if that boundary is broken and the rewards if the boundary is kept. Have your teen sign this "contract" to ensure she understands the seriousness of the issue. Tell her that should another unexcused absence occur, it will result in more serious repercussions, such as notifying the police. Friendship privileges may be revoked if skipping classes continues with the same person.

You might also choose to meet with the parents of the other student in order to strategize a joint confrontation and consistent repercussions. A meeting held with other parents is a personal choice and a good one if you know them. Most school officials will remove themselves from meeting with multiple parents in one setting, as they prefer to focus on one student at a time.

Wisdom from King Solomon says, "Two are better than one, because they have a good reward for their toil" (Eccles. 4:9).

WHAT COULD YOU SAY?

Once you have all the information you can get your hands on, sit down for a heart-to-heart with your daughter. You might say, "Bethany, I have to be honest with you about how disappointed I am over this. I view skipping school as very serious for three reasons. First, you've violated my trust and the trust of your teachers. Second, you have violated your own conscience. Third, you have demonstrated a form of deception, and I consider any deception to be troubling and unacceptable.

"You know how much I love you. But you will no longer have the maneuvering room to be deceptive. The school has been instructed that unless I call confirming your legitimate absence, they will call me immediately upon discovering that you are not in class. Then I will alert the police to search for you as a truant, and I will take off work myself to go look for you.

"Moreover, you are grounded from all social activities for six weeks. I know you want me to trust you, and I sincerely want to trust you. But you are the only one who can earn back the trust that has been lost. I love you too much to do nothing about this. I am confident you will restore my trust in you." Let your teen know you want to be able to say as Paul did, "I rejoice, because I have perfect confidence in you" (2 Cor. 7:16).

WISDOM FROM GOD'S WORD

Do not feel guilty about putting limits on your teenager's social activities. The limits you enforce are born out of your love.

Better is open rebuke than hidden love. (Prov. 27:5)

18

Missing Homework

"Oh, by the way . . ." These are the words no parent wants to hear from their teens, especially after 8:00 at night. "Oh, by the way, a science project is due tomorrow." For starters, this is *not* the reason some stores are open 24/7.

It's the last week of the semester. You've been asking your teens all semester for progress reports, and you've been getting "thumbs up." Now they are frantic, asking you for help in order to pass two classes.

So what is a parent to do? You want your teens to do well in school. Do you *rescue* or *refuse to help*?

HOMEWORK IS THEIR JOB

School *is* the job of our teens. It is developmentally appropriate for them to complain about having excessive homework and not enough time to get it all done. A parent is always wise to get an objective analysis of the situation. But factors other than too much homework may need to be addressed.

In this situation it would be helpful to do a quick inventory of your teens' time-on-task behaviors. Are they listening to their iPods? Is the cell phone nearby, creating the temptation to text? The computer may be used for school assignments, but it also makes it easy for teens to "take a break" to surf the Net or "chat" with their friends. Remove any device that would hinder or become a distraction or a temptation for teens to socialize rather than work.

Even for one with the greatest powers of focus and concentration, it would be hard to accomplish work under these conditions. The fact that the organization center in the brain of teenagers isn't fully developed can lead the teen to *think* that countless hours are being consumed with endless homework while in reality more time is spent socializing than studying.

Extracurricular activities may be another reason your teens aren't finishing all of their homework. Many teens are involved in athletics, music, drama, or competitions outside the classroom as well as in church activities. Adding homework to that schedule can be extremely challenging.

As a parent, you have the difficult role of determining when to help and when not to help in order to avoid enabling and rescuing your teen. Much of this decision will be based on how well you know your teens' strengths and weaknesses, along with the foundation you have laid for learning.

Learning issues may be a factor with some teens. They may require more time to do their work or specialized training in how to study. Others may need a tutor.

Do your teens understand that homework is their job, their responsibility? Have you helped create healthy homework habits? Is excessive homework a result of not using their time wisely at school? What is the real issue when it comes to homework?

MOVING FROM HOMEWORK HASSLES TO HEALTHY HOMEWORK HABITS

As a well-meaning parent, you may have purchased a study desk and lamp for your student teen, thinking, *Now we will start seeing some better grades*. You may return later only to find your teen sprawled on the bed, surrounded by textbooks, papers strewn everywhere on the floor, and music blaring. The only activity that has occurred at the desk has been the tossing of various items onto it.

Or the desk has become an electronic media center, and your teen is using it to manage media functions. You notice the computer is being used for maintaining social networks, music, and instant messaging—or worse yet, for gambling. The nearby cell phone is ever-ready to send and receive texts, and the desk conveniently houses video games. In frustration, you throw up your hands and wonder, *What is a parent to do?*

Varied learning styles require different ways to study. The most effective thing parents can do is to help their teens understand their individual learning styles and how to study accordingly. Proverbs 22:6 (AMP) says, "Train up a child in the way he should go [*and in keeping with his individual gift or bent*]" (italics added).

Because your teens may learn in different ways, you can optimize success in study time by making some adaptations to the way they do their homework. Teens like to feel that you trust them to get the job done. Instead of allowing homework to become a power struggle, empower them by giving choices to help them study in ways that are more consistent with their learning style.

WHAT COULD YOU DO?

- Set boundaries.
  - A designated homework time.
  - Designate a place to do homework. If your teens cannot work independently, sitting near you may be the best option.
  - Choose a predetermined way for you to monitor progress. You want your teens to see you as a support, not a nag. Talk ahead of time about what works best. Then follow through with a positive attitude.
  - Allow no electronic gadgets during homework time (except that which is absolutely necessary to complete the assignment).
- Create a system for rewards.
  - Rewards can be given in the form of breaks. Teens are very good at appearing busy for a long period of time. Base breaks on the number of tasks accomplished rather than on the amount of time spent.
  - Clearly define what activities are acceptable during the breaks. They can get something to eat, call or text a friend, and/or do something physical.
  - Break time is not a good time to play video games. It is very hard to get teens back on task for homework.
  - A ten- to fifteen-minute break should be sufficient.
- Determine a system for repercussions if the homework guidelines are not followed.
  - A short-term repercussion might be given for not staying on task. You determine the most effective consequence for not following established guidelines.
  - A long-term repercussion is appropriate when grades fall below a mutually agreed-upon standard. A healthy and realistic assessment of their abilities is very important. You may have to cut back on their social life until there is evidence of improvement.
- Establish clear boundaries with homework.
  - If your teens' school has online access to grades, check them often.

— As mentioned earlier, remove any device that may present a distraction.
— Check homework before your teens go to bed.
— You may need to quiz them before big exams.

Remember, your role as a parent is to equip, encourage, and empower—not to enable.

WHAT COULD YOU SAY?

To make sure your teens know that homework *is* their job, communicate this in a matter-of-fact manner. "This is the platform that prepares you for the rest of your life, and that is why it is important. School is the learning center, and homework is the practice training. God's Word applies so beautifully here, as God tells us: 'Whatever you do, work at it with all your heart, as working for the Lord, not for men' (Col. 3:23 NIV). I believe in you and in your ability to learn. Let's find out what works best for the way your brain is wired.

"We have looked at how you learn and have made some adjustments in how you can do your homework. We did this in order to help you do better and thus experience more success in school. If you choose not to take this responsibility seriously, you will forfeit time with your cell phone and friends. If you choose to use what you have learned to make wise decisions, you will have the joy of experiencing more success in school, and also we will extend your social privileges."

If you have a global learner who feels overwhelmed, the following words will be a healing balm: "I know it seems like a mountain of work to do. Let's try to *eat this elephant* one bite at a time. What do you have for first period? Let's write it down." Continue to help your student see the small component parts instead of only the *whole*.

You may want to sit down with your teens in a neutral environment, perhaps over food, and announce that you are going to allow them individually to set up their learning environment. You may say, "I care about you and your grades. More importantly, I care that you are learning. Therefore, I am going to let you set up your study environment in a way that works for your learning style. We will be able to tell if it is working by the success you have in doing your homework. This is a privilege. If you abuse it, you'll lose it. I have faith you will use it wisely."

If you experience success in the first step but your teen needs additional support, you can move to this next step by asking questions such as:

- Do you learn better when people are around or when you are alone?
- Do you prefer to study in the den with the family there, in the den when the family is not around, or alone in your room?
- Does it help when I quiz you before a test?
- Do you remember better when you see it or when you talk about it?
- Does it help you to move when you study? You can try sitting on an exercise ball and gently moving as you study. See if the physical movement helps you retain information.

Be diligent to equip and empower your teens to find what works best, and then encourage them to do it. Being successful in school and in life is simply finding what works and then doing it. Your teens will feel encouraged by your trust.

WISDOM FROM GOD'S WORD

God tells us that His Word and commandments are the most important things we will ever teach anyone. Yet He shows us clearly that we are to teach His truths in different ways. When you provide these different avenues for your teens to learn, homework can be a more positive experience, and they can begin to enjoy the learning process.

> These words that I command you today shall be on your heart. You shall teach them diligently to your children, and shall talk of them when you sit in your house, and when you walk by the way, and when you lie down, and when you rise. You shall bind them as a sign on your hand, and they shall be as frontlets between your eyes. You shall write them on the doorposts of your house and on your gates. (Deut. 6:6–9)

19

Failing Grades

Your daughter Diane began the school year with optimism. But as her enthusiasm waned and her grades sank, you found yourself floundering in a sea of dismay. Time and again you reminded her to do her homework, but to no avail. And unless the problem is corrected, Diane will fail.

WHAT COULD YOU DO?

A parent-teacher conference is essential to probe for reasons homework is not being done. Is your daughter committed to too many activities? If so, something will have to go. Does she not understand the material? If so, tutoring may help. Or is the homework just not a priority? If so, an accountability system will need to be put in place. Solicit feedback from the teacher about your teen's behavior during class.

Talk with your teen to get her perspective. Suggest she propose a solution and discuss it with you. Kids can be quite creative when challenged. This may work—it may not. Bottom line, your teen needs to learn to manage time and prioritize daily. Obviously you have the option of tying privileges to finished homework, such as no TV or cell phone until homework assignments are completed *to your satisfaction.*

You might designate a specific time for doing homework—allowing no phone calls, no visits, no interruptions of any kind. You may need to be the homework monitor for a while. Find out her assignments, when tests are coming up, and what needs to be studied. Help your daughter pace herself. Search your memory for motivators that helped you do your schoolwork.

Identify your teen's academic strengths and weaknesses. For instance, because I love puzzles, I liked ninth grade algebra. Figuring out the equations was like putting a puzzle together. What helped me most was having homework to do every day. It provided my daily impetus for studying. In other subjects like history, we didn't have daily assignments, so I had greater difficulty. If we had few tests covering many chapters throughout the semester, I had a hard time pacing myself.

Break large assignments or tests down into small, bite-sized chunks. (As the old saying goes, "You eat an elephant one bite at a time!") Discovering your teen's learning style will provide a clue as to what kind of help is needed.

Another common reason for failure, especially among bright or gifted students, is *burnout*. These youngsters go into accelerated programs where they are expected to master more difficult subject matter than their peers.

Each year the pressure to achieve increases, culminating in very competitive high school programs designed to garner scholarships from even more competitive universities. Tragically, the suicide rate among high-achieving students indicates how intolerable the stress can be.

Parents would do well to be wary of too many programs, too many competitions, too much pushing. Watch your teen for signs of stress—difficulty sleeping or sleeping too much, irritability, withdrawal, self-injury, constant anxiety, or unhealthy eating habits (ranging from consuming excessive junk food to severely limited eating as in anorexia or bulimia). If you see these signs, reevaluate your teen's activities.

Offer the option to drop some activities; then observe the reaction. Even scaling back can help. One mother candidly commented, "My daughter has always excelled in English. So I was floored when she wanted to drop honors English during her junior year. I opened my mouth to absolutely forbid it when the Lord reminded me, 'You dropped honors algebra your junior year of high school.' I had indeed, and it saved my sanity. So I told her she could."

Sometimes teens struggle with grades when they experience heartache. Tenth grade was the worst year of my life. I chose to confront my father about his infidelity and was sent off to boarding school. One quarter that year, I failed all of my classes except one in which I got a D. I wasn't focused on school. I wasn't focused on friends. My focus was on my mother's need for protection, and my heart was in the deepest despair.

I appreciated that my mom didn't scold me about my grades. I knew she cared most about my heart. And since neither of us knew what to do about our home situation, we both struggled. Fortunately, along the way I became an authentic Christian, and my changed life in Christ changed my heart and changed my perspective.

For a few months that year I had a tutor—a wonderful, nonjudgmental woman who made me feel valued and assured me that somehow I'd make it through. I never shared personal details of my life with her, but I felt that if I wanted to I could confide in her. I knew she cared about me. Her caring heart helped beyond measure.

One of the greatest gifts you can give your teens is to help them understand their God-given personality and learning style. When teens are floundering and failing, they tend to lose sight of the fact that every person has both strengths and weaknesses. If your teen learns better through moving and doing and touching, encourage consideration of an occupation involving physical movement. If your teen considers school the avenue for achieving personal goals, her perspective about study will change as she works with her own learning style. Perhaps she could study while sitting on an exercise ball.

If your teen likes to talk as well as listen, encourage consideration of a profession that involves speaking. Rather than talking in class and being disruptive, your teen can channel that desire into future career opportunities.

Teens generally cannot see beyond *now*. As you help them understand how God wired them for His purpose, you give them a window to see their future. They need to know, "Now is not forever; the best is yet to come." Sometimes a change in study methods results in improved grades. Those with a *learning difference*—such as dyslexia or *ADHD*—may need specialized support. Have your teen professionally tested to see whether a learning disability is the culprit. Help your teen know with certainty, as King David did, "The LORD will fulfill his purpose for me" (Ps. 138:8).

WHAT COULD YOU SAY?

If your teenager is motivated with hope, she can learn almost anything. Not long ago I met a high school student thoroughly discouraged over how poorly she was doing in math. I told her, "I know something that can make a huge difference. Would you be willing to devote a weekend beginning Saturday morning to tackle math?"

"Anything," Kris replied desperately. "I cannot flunk this class."

"Then start back at the front of the book. Read every word on every page at the beginning, where the book explains the foundational concepts. At the end of each chapter there is always a test. You'll love it because they'll be a snap. Make sure to work each problem so you understand the principle. Work your way through the book exercise by exercise. You will actually come to understand algebra." With only the tiniest mustard seed of hope, she promised to try.

I later received a letter from Kris, telling me ecstatically that she had brought her grade up from a D to an A! She had thought she was stupid, that she would always struggle and never understand the principles behind the problems. But this simple study method enabled her to capture the concepts she had missed.

I learned this study method by watching my college roommate. Both of us were studying Italian. She had an A average. My grade had slipped to a C+ going into the final exam. When I saw Linda go back to the beginning of the book and do the language exercises page by page, I did the same. To my amazement, I made a 98 on the final exam and earned an A for the semester.

If you have a teenager struggling to "make the grade," emphasize this: "For the remainder of this six weeks, your social activities on school nights, including talking on the cell phone and time on the computer, are suspended unless it is related to homework. Every night you are to spend a minimum of two hours studying, then review with me what you've done before getting ready for bed. Once you have improved your grades, you can gradually resume your social activities as long as you keep your grades up. You are smart, so we must find a way for you to study smart. I want you to give serious thought to why your grades have dropped and to come up with a plan for bringing them back up. We'll sit down after dinner and discuss it. It's going to take effort, but with God's help you can do it." Psalm 28:7 says, "The LORD is my strength and my shield; in him my heart trusts, and I am helped."

WISDOM FROM GOD'S WORD

Take the pressure off your teen by explaining that if she does her best, she will please both you and God.

> Whatever you do, work heartily, as for the Lord and not for men. (Col. 3:23)

Additional related resources (audio and print) are available from Hope for the Heart (http://www.hopefortheheart.org/):

Success through Failure

20
Cheating

While your son is gone, his friend calls for the page numbers of a history assignment. When you open your son's binder to locate the assignment, you discover a homework paper clearly not his. Your heart sinks as you study the paper. Did Collin really copy someone else's homework? Has he been cheating?

Cheating has reached epidemic proportions ranging from illegally downloading music to texting information on an exam, from taking performance-enhancing drugs to downloading research papers. The more often teens succumb to these enticements, the more often boundary lines between right and wrong are blurred.

A far larger percentage of today's high school and college students cheat on their schoolwork than ever. Reasons may range from decreasing moral standards to increasing competition for scholarships and from pressure to achieve to availability of cheating "tools."

Interestingly, the students who most frequently cheat already make high grades. They cheat with the hope of graduating with top honors. However, dishonest grades only reap dishonor.

Plagiarism, considered an academic crime, is also on the rise and must be taken seriously. Teachers often use Web sites and software that are specifically designed to track whether or not their students are cheating.

Sadly, while the number of teens who cheat grows, most teens indicate that they are not dissatisfied with their integrity. They feel justified with techno-cheating simply because the information is available. They fail to realize that with this wealth of information comes the enormous responsibility to handle it in a Christlike manner. "One who is faithful in a very little is also faithful in much, and one who is dishonest in a very little is also dishonest in much" (Luke 16:10).

WHAT COULD YOU DO?

First, find out whether your teen *is* actually cheating. What one teacher may consider cheating, another may encourage, viewing it as "cooperative homework." If you observe homework being shared, you might ask, "Do you think you are learning that material well enough for a test?"

- Confidence says, "Oh, sure, no problem."
- Embarrassment says, "Uh, I hope so."
- Defensiveness says, "Yes, so leave me alone!"

Listen to the reaction. It could be an indication of whether or not your teen is cutting corners with homework. If so, the best "teacher" may be the repercussions that come at test time . . . unless, of course, cheating happens on the test.

Although you can't monitor the class, most teachers who catch students cheating give automatic zeros on the assignment. Notice any unexplained zeros on your teen's progress reports. Most school discipline plans have a cheating policy. It would be to your advantage to know what to expect each time a student cheats.

Another option is to give your teen a quiz and review information the evening before scheduled tests. If he is consistently ill-prepared, consider reviewing his homework on a daily basis. One mother confided, "Chris does not test well. Even when he knows the material, he gets so uptight during tests that he feels compelled to glance at other nearby papers. When his seventh-grade teacher noticed what he was doing, she just turned his chair around to face the wall. He came home embarrassed enough to decide he was going to change. Before his next test, I went over and over the material with him until he knew it backward and forward. As a result, he wasn't so tempted to 'peek.'"

Regarding class participation, speak with your teen's teachers. Ask for suggestions about how to help teenagers at home. After consulting with the teacher, consider all of your options. One of the best ways to help them overcome a dependence on plagiarism is to be their accountability partner. Keep yourself informed regarding all reports they will need to complete. Help them establish and follow through on a reading schedule. This will prepare your teenagers for their written reports. Additionally, you could:

- Engage them in conversation regarding what they are reading.
- Review with them the class notes or textbook.
- Give them a quiz over the material.
- Have them read their paper to you or give you a copy to read yourself before turning it in.

Make it clear to your teens that their job is to be the best student they can possibly be. Challenge your teens to learn all they can. Encourage them to maintain their integrity in the classroom so they will have a clear conscience and will be a good witness to their classmates. Explain that cheating is equivalent to stealing. Spiritually, cheating will hinder their prayers and block the favor of God on their life. Psalm 5:12 says, "You bless the righteous, O LORD; you cover him with favor as with a shield."

WHAT COULD YOU SAY?

"You know I love you and always want the best for you. While cheating on homework or a test may seem insignificant to you, cheating is very significant to God and to me. I realize your goal is to get a good grade, and that's an appropriate goal. But you can't pass God's test on integrity if you cheat in school. Your grades count for this present time, but your integrity counts for eternity.

"God is far more concerned that you have Christlike character than that you have great grades. My responsibility as a parent is to see that you have the same priority. So for now, all of your social privileges are suspended until you settle this matter of integrity for yourself and then decide how you'll demonstrate to me that it is settled. I know that in the deepest part of your heart you want to live a life of integrity. I'm more than willing to help you any way that I can." Then have your teen make a possible plan and discuss it with you.

If there is another incident with cheating on his schoolwork, he will need to make proper restitution. For example,

- You will apologize to your teacher in person as well as in writing.
- You will be grounded from activities in order to allow more time for studying.
- You can expect me to check on your schoolwork regularly.
- If there is plagiarism, you will write to the person from whom you got the information and ask for his or her forgiveness as well as receive any penalties if some are given.

WISDOM FROM GOD'S WORD

Give your teenagers the following proverb, which in regard to cheating presents both a reward and a repercussion. Then ask them to read it each night just before turning off the light.

> The integrity of the upright guides them, but the crookedness of the treacherous destroys them. (Prov. 11:3)

21

Bullying

You receive a message from your daughter's school to "come to the office immediately." Every thought imaginable races through your mind. *Is she sick? Was there an accident? Was she hurt? Is she in trouble?* As you pull up to the school, an ambulance is pulling away. You search frantically for a parking place and *rush* into the school office, where another mother sobs as the administrator relays a heartbreaking story.

"As you know, Mrs. Jones's daughter, Anna, is the flyer on the cheerleading squad—the one on top of the pyramid.

"It appears that some of the other cheerleaders are jealous of her and 'accidentally' failed to catch her during a stunt this morning. Anna suffered a broken collarbone and will be sidelined for the season. From the information we are receiving, it was a premeditated, malicious act intended to 'eliminate the competition,' and it was contrived and spearheaded by your daughter."

You sit there stunned and horrified, torn between anger at your daughter, anger at yourself for not acting on obvious warning signals, anger with the situation, and deep sadness for Anna and her mother. Frankly, you don't know what to say. Tears of anger, shame, sadness, fear, and frustration run down your face.

WHAT COULD YOU DO?

"Bullying is a deliberate hostile physical or verbal activity intended to harm, induce fear and create terror."[1] Those who are bullied live with continual fear and expectation of future harassment . . . or they themselves become bullies to stop the pain.[2]

Bullies normally exploit someone who is perceived to be weaker physically or psychologically. They delight in causing pain and receive a sense of reward, significance, or gratification from abusing others.

Cyber-bullying has become the latest way to harass and hurt others through e-mail, instant messaging, texting, and social networking. The pressure of adolescence compounded with these additional stresses can lead to tragedy. *Bully-cide* is the new label that describes those who have been so continually bullied that they resort to suicide.

Educate yourself about girl bullies. They are:

- perceived as fickle *bully-princesses* seeking power
- physically aggressive and mean
- emotionally manipulative and deceptive
- socially willing to seek and destroy anyone considered weaker, superior, threatening, or disliked
- a clique of girl bullies empowering group members and exerting a great deal of control over others

Educate yourself about boy bullies. They are:

- perceived as *bully-gangsters* seeking power
- physically violent
- emotionally lacking in empathy, with a sense of entitlement
- socially ready to hurt anyone who is considered inferior, vulnerable, disabled, annoying, or different in any way
- a gang of male bullies empowering and controlling each other

For more on this, see chapter 22, "Fighting," and chapter 41, "Violence."

In regard to the cheerleading scenario, some bullies' actions have escalated to a potentially life-endangering situation. Swift action must be taken.

- Initiate immediate intervention, including speaking with the school counselor and the police regarding intervention programs available for teens.
- Establish boundaries that are unquestionably fair, clearly communicated, and consistently enforced in a respectful manner.
- Provide repercussions that not only relate to the offense but retrain behavior, are restorative in nature, and are relative to the degree of repentance.
- Reinforce responsible behavior by rewarding it with verbal acknowledgments and praise, and with increased responsibilities and privileges.
- Seek to establish a safe, bully-free environment in your own home by cultivating a spirit in your family that says, "I love you, trust you, hear you, value you, respect you, believe in you, and am here for you."
- Set a zero-tolerance level on bullying by holding your teen accountable for offensive behaviors, enforcing appropriate repercussions related to any offenses, and providing opportunities for your teen to make restitution.

- Monitor aggressive video games, movies and television programs, social relationships, music and music videos.
- Model kindness and consideration, express unconditional love, and listen attentively.

You will need to take steps to both protect your teens and promote healing. Bullying can escalate quickly. Your goal is not only to train them how to handle conflict constructively and how to get help in serious situations but also how to develop compassion and empathy.

Watch for signs that your teen is *being bullied*. These include:

- wanting to miss school
- withdrawing from social activities
- eating too little or too much
- experiencing general anxiety, fear, and/or depression
- engaging in extreme self-destructive behaviors
- receiving threatening e-mails or visiting suspicious Web sites

Take action in the case of *cyber-bullying*.

- Use parental controls and filtering, software, and/or online tracking programs.
- Offer to look at their communications with them, make copies of threatening correspondence for your files, and ."delete" together so your teens know that you are there for them. Talk and pray as you go. (Before "deleting," communicate all cyber-bullying to the school.)

Look for signs that your teen is *bullying others*.

- Listen to conversations your teen has with friends.
- Be aware of your teen's demeanor.
- Notice the kind of clothing being worn. (All one color is often a sign of involvement with a clique, posse, or gang; all black typically represents the occult and/or Satanism.)
- Pay attention to the way your teen wears a hat.
- Look for any marks on your teen's body.
- Note any recurring doodling or drawings.
- Check out e-mails, text messages, and Web site participation.

Enforce repercussions if your teen is a bully.

- Find a time and place to talk with your teen in private.
- Pray, ponder, and plan what you are going to say.
- State your concerns in a calm manner.
- Settle on repercussions that are specific, swift, and relevant to the offense.

- Make the heart of your teen your highest priority. If there is sincere remorse with a repentant heart, a plan of redemption can include restitution with those being bullied.
- Help your teen make a list of specific acts of kindness that can be done for those who have been offended. Pray that God will turn your teen's heart toward him and others.
- Arrange a meeting between you, your teen, the injured teen, and his or her parents. Show your teen how Jesus wants us to resolve hurts in person, not via e-mails, texts, or phone calls. Meeting with the injured person face-to-face will give your teen opportunity to see the other teen's pain and begin to develop sensitivity and empathy.
- Reward desired attitudes and actions with words of praise, appreciation, and encouragement and through increased trust.

If you have teenage boys, help them learn how to use their words to resolve conflict rather than to create more conflict with physical confrontations. Help your teenage girls break the bullying patterns of gossip, meanness, cliques, and aggression by providing long-term mentoring. Teach them biblical patterns for communication, and reward responsible behavior with increased freedom and words of encouragement and praise. Realize the wisdom of Proverbs 9:12 (NIV): "If you are wise, your wisdom will reward you; if you are a mocker, you alone will suffer."

WHAT COULD YOU SAY?

If your teenaged daughter is being a *bully*, you might confront her with the truth and with her need to change. "Years ago, my heart went out to you because I knew you were being bullied. It was so unjust. Later I saw you learn to resist pressure and you developed endurance. Now you've come to a time in your life when you are doing what was done to you. You don't want to hurt, so you've chosen ways to hurt others. If you continue to hurt others, you'll never have peace within your heart. I love you too much to stand back and do nothing. I've arranged for us to talk with someone who understands the kind of pain you're in and how to bring true hope to your heart.

"This situation is so serious because you have literally brought harm to others. This meeting is essential—I care too much about you to not do this. If you decide not to go with me, then all privileges will be removed—no car, no allowance, no phone—nothing. Our first meeting is Saturday morning at 10:00. Although this will take real work, I'm actually excited about the healing you will receive and the future that God has for you. I love you."

WISDOM FROM GOD'S WORD

Teens can be either bullies or be bullied in various ways. Either role always begins in their hearts. Spend time with your teens in order to help them understand that their words and actions come from the overflow of their hearts. When their hearts are right with the Lord, everything else will follow.

> Search me, O God, and know my heart! Try me and know my thoughts! And see if there be any grievous way in me, and lead me in the way everlasting! (Ps. 139:23–24)

Additional related resources (audio and print) are available from Hope for the Heart (http://www.hopefortheheart.org/):

Verbal & Emotional Abuse; Victimization; Confrontation; Anger; Fear; Rejection; Prejudice

22

Fighting

What a shock! Your son initiated a fight and bloodied the nose of another student! The school nurse treated the other boy, and the school resource officer filed a police report. Now you have to pick up your son, who is suspended until you can meet with the principal.

WHAT COULD YOU DO?

Your best response is to set up the school conference as soon as possible. Although you will talk to your son about what happened and may even feel a certain sympathy for him, this is not the time to come to his rescue. He must learn that striking out in anger hurts himself more than anyone else and results in undesirable repercussions.

Fights rarely happen out of the blue. Most likely, a precipitating situation has been simmering for some time. The other boy could have provoked your son with taunts or teasing, shoving, or profanity. As you discuss the situation with the school officials, listen attentively to their appraisal of the situation, including their recommendations for resolution. Above all, your teen must take full responsibility for what he did. If it makes him angry because he doesn't feel responsible, privately explain how his attempt to resolve the matter with violence has rendered you powerless to defend him.

Regardless of other factors, he had choices he simply did not exercise. Most likely, he will not seriously consider any of these choices in the future unless he experiences a painful repercussion in the present.

If possible, a face-to-face meeting with the other boy and his parents is desirable. Your son must offer a sincere apology and pay any medical expenses. A penitent attitude can go a long way toward improving legal ramifications. It is doubtful anyone will want to drag you to court or see your son in jail. What will be wanted is an apology and assurance that it won't happen again. The apology should greatly help in clearing the air between the two combatants, and if the adults demonstrate peacemaking, more than likely the teens will follow suit.

Many teenagers have been jailed, and many a loving parent has waited to post bail. A painful ordeal can provide a powerful turnaround in the life of troubled teens.

Your teen must complete, with a reasonably good attitude, whatever disciplinary action is required of him. (And if you are right there with him mowing yards, he might surprise you with his overt willingness to do it.)

All his social functions should be suspended immediately. His free time at home is to be spent writing down all the options he could have chosen when he felt angry. Meanwhile, make your own list. Then, at a regular time each week, get together and talk about any feelings of anger he has had and about his positive options. Be quick to acknowledge and praise him for the times he chooses one of those positive options rather than a negative one. Rewarding positive behavior with a verbal affirmation or a physical pat on the back both reinforces and encourages such behavior. Use this time to build a stronger relationship with him.

If the fight resulted from gang activity, you have another problem altogether. Gangs are spreading everywhere like wildfire. The sense of belonging, of empowerment, of secrecy, and of living on the edge tends to make kids who feel disenfranchised vulnerable to the lure of gang membership. Be sure to have a zero-tolerance policy when it comes to gang activity. School resource officers are very helpful when you need legal information regarding gang violence.

Don't assume your teen could never be drawn into gang activity. If your son spends a lot of time away from home with undesirable friends or continually wears certain clothing and unfamiliar emblems or assumes a different dialect, stance, or gestures, be forewarned. You may need to play Sherlock Holmes to discover his level of involvement. Talk to him, but don't be surprised if he won't respond—loyalty is a primary attribute of gang membership. You will need help from the school resource officer or your police department's gang unit to find out what gangs you're dealing with, how dangerous they are, and who the rival gangs are. (See chapter 41, "Violence," for more information.)

Set the example as a parent of *acting* rather than *reacting* in situations where your anger is provoked. "If it is possible, as far as it depends on you, live at peace with everyone" (Rom. 12:18 NIV).

Take measures to make your teen understand his worth and his unique role as a family member. Grounding a young man involved in gang activities may be futile—you will have to move or he will have to come to the decision himself that this lifestyle is not for him. It may be helpful to attend sessions with a gang counselor who can show your son morgue photos of gang warfare casualties. Above all, remember the power of spiritual warfare. Pray diligently, and look for the Lord's deliverance.

WHAT COULD YOU SAY?

"Son, I'm standing by you, no matter what. I know you had a legitimate right to be upset. If you had gone to the coach or any school official or even to me about your problem with this boy, we could have done something to help you. But losing control as you did just makes you come across as the bad guy. Now people see you as a bigger problem than he is! What do you think would happen if I handled a troublemaker at my office like you did? I'd be arrested, spend time in jail, lose my job, and be unable to provide for our family.

"We all feel anger at times. Being angry is not the problem. How you expressed your anger is the problem. Your anger was out of control. No matter what someone does to provoke you, you need to keep control of *you*. Does it feel good for you to be out of control?" (He'll probably say no.)

"One of the basic tenets in the martial arts describes the relationship between self-respect and self-control: *He cannot respect himself if he cannot control himself.*

"I'm committed to helping you grow in the areas of self-respect and self-control, which Galatians 5:23 says you'll have when you're filled with God's Spirit. Right now, because you are having difficulty displaying self-control and are a threat to others, you leave me no choice but to restrict your time with others after school and on weekends. All social functions are suspended until I feel confident you can control yourself. I am committed to helping you learn the value of acting responsibly toward people, and I'll do whatever it takes to help you do that."

WISDOM FROM GOD'S WORD

Fighting and all other forms of violence erupt out of unresolved anger. Help your teens see that God calls out-of-control anger "sin"—an anger over which they *can* have control.

> Be angry, and do not sin; ponder in your own hearts on your beds, and be silent. (Ps. 4:4)

Additional related resources (audio and print) are available from Hope for the Heart (http://www.hopefortheheart.org/):

Conflict Resolution

23

Sexual Harassment

Your normally outgoing daughter has suddenly become anxious and withdrawn. She's reluctant to go to school and reluctant to talk about what's bothering her. Mary's fearful behavior is quite unlike her. When you press for an explanation, she ashamedly admits that Jason has been sexually harassing her at school.

WHAT COULD YOU DO?

Teenage girls and boys alike can harass others sexually and can be harassed. Students are sexually harassed in many ways—physically, through the Internet, cell phones, or text messaging, and on Web sites. Technology has propelled sexual harassment and parenting to a new level. Any unwelcome conduct of a sexual nature constitutes sexual harassment.

Many teens are placing themselves in danger without realizing it. They send sexually explicit text messages with sexual photographs to each other's cell phones. They take pictures of each other and post them on Web sites. What seems a harmless prank to some is actually sexual harassment and even criminal pornography. Teens are no longer safe even in the confines of their own homes.

Teen dating violence is also a growing epidemic and is defined as intentional physical, sexual, verbal, or emotional abuse in order to *harm*, *threaten*, *intimidate*, *or control* another person in a dating relationship. Most teens have experienced dangerous dating or know someone who has.[1] And much of the abuse occurs in school buildings or on school grounds.[2]

Common clues to look for include:

- physical injury
- change in mood or personality
- falling grades

• use of drugs/alcohol
• isolation
• excessive texting
• excessive instant messaging
• emotional outbursts

WHAT COULD YOU DO?

If your teen is being harassed, your first challenge is simply to find out exactly what has happened. Your teen's willingness to talk with you about something so intimately painful can strengthen your relationship. Treat what your teens say very seriously, and encourage them to be specific.

Ask:

• Who was involved?
• What was said?
• What was done?
• How did you respond?
• Where did it happen?
• What were the circumstances?
• How often has it happened?
• Was anyone else around?
• If so, who?
• Whom have you told?
• What are your fears?
• What are you feeling toward the harasser?
• How are you feeling about yourself?

Take notes on everything said.

Do not give any guarantees of keeping your teen's story a secret. Emphasize that due to the seriousness of the situation, you must report the misconduct to school administrators, who are legally required to investigate such reports in a fair, complete manner. Prepare your teen to expect aggressive questioning, especially if the accusation is about a faculty or staff member. Any perceived inconsistencies or apparent falsehoods in responses will cast serious doubts on your teen's credibility.

Warn them not to make up something just to fill in what they can't remember. Once the authorities are involved, there's no turning back. Therefore, they are to speak only about that of which they are certain.

It may be that your teen does not want to make an official complaint.

Many kids brought up to be polite, cooperative, and trusting are totally unprepared to deal with abusive or offensive behavior from others. But the world is a battle zone in which Christians, both male and female, are required to display courage, intelligence, and resourcefulness in order to stand against ungodly onslaughts. For this reason it may actually be preferable that your teenagers handle the reporting themselves. However, if the offender is an adult, you are legally required to inform the authorities, and you will need to be a strong supporter for your teen.

While anyone can become a victim of harassment, consider whether your teen's behavior could be fueling the situation. Sometimes wearing revealing clothing or too much makeup or inappropriate jewelry or maintaining a helpless or vulnerable demeanor could embolden an abuser. However, nothing justifies abusing another person.

Along with your teen, evaluate whether your teen is sending harmful signals and not realizing it. Without accusing or blaming, make certain your son or daughter sees how he or she could be contributing to being a target. While inappropriate dress does not excuse inappropriate actions on the part of others, your teens must take responsibility for the image they project. Teens who try to dress like sex symbols or pop stars should not be surprised when others respond sexually.

Evaluate how your teens are viewed.

• Are they extremely shy and timid, walking with head down, avoiding eye contact, books clutched to their chest?
• Are they hesitant to speak up in class when they know the answers?
• Are they constantly apologizing?

If these apply, then in the twisted thinking of many emotionally immature individuals, your son or daughter is asking for harassment. Let them know that abusers look for those whom they can successfully abuse. Help your teens walk and talk confidently. Coach them in walking with their heads up (without making eye contact with harassers), shoulders back, and with strong strides. Show them how to carry their books in a less vulnerable manner. Teach them to respond to verbal attacks with a silent but steady glare. They need not undergo a personality change; they just need to develop backbone.

If your teenaged son is doing the harassing, you may not know anything about it until you are contacted by his school. Then, after you have recovered from the shock, talk with him to find out *exactly* what is going on. Ask the five Ws: who? where? what? when? and why?

Some boys do not know how to approach a girl without harassing or stalking her. If grown men have trouble ascertaining the level of a female's interest—and some do—it's much harder for a teenager. In fact, her interest is the crucial factor: if she's interested, he's flirting; if she's not interested, he's harassing. Compounding this difficulty is the fact that the girl does not have to tell the boy that he is offending her for his behavior to be considered harassment. All she has to do is tell someone else.

If the harassment was unintentional and your son is remorseful and/ or embarrassed by the girl's reaction, then tutor him in how to read subtle, conflicting female signals. If a girl makes a complaint, he must absolutely leave her alone. He must not talk to her, look at her, or talk *about* her to other people at school. If he does, it can be considered retaliation and cause him even greater trouble. In the future, if he is interested in a girl, suggest that he visualize himself driving down a street through a series of intersections where *she* controls the stoplights. If he comes to a red light, he must stop. He cannot proceed. If he gets a green light, he can proceed, but only to the next intersection—he cannot continue to barrel through every intersection.

The first traffic light is eye contact and facial expression. When he is around her or speaks to her, does she make eye contact with him? Does she smile at him? If she does neither, that's a red light. He may attempt to converse with her about school, but he must not try to go beyond that. If she does make eye contact and smile, that does not mean she is in love with him. She could simply be a naturally friendly person. But he nonetheless has a green light to the next intersection, which is proximity and general attitude.

- If he attempts to stand close enough to her to whisper (for example), does she let him stay there, or does she back away?
- Does she linger to talk to him, or does she turn her back to him and talk to someone else?
- Does she initiate conversation with him?
- Does she write him notes?
- Does she touch him?

If all these are green lights, he can assume she enjoys his company, and he can continue down this road within appropriate boundaries.

Part of your job as a parent is to make sure he understands that he is not to proceed automatically through any intersections that lead to more personal territory. Remind him that lights can change from green to red, and he must stop when they do. If he is mature enough, he can ask her why, but he should know that persistence in trying to change matters can lead to charges of harassment. However, if he has been watchful at the intersections, he will have seen a caution sign warning of a road closure ahead.

If you discover that your son has been harassing a girl just for the sake of harassment, *then* you can enact repercussions on him because such behavior is indefensible. Lecture all you want about respect for others and how his behavior reflects on you, but be aware of the other factors at work, specifically his friends. This kind of behavior usually happens for the benefit of an "audience." So when you are questioning him, be sure to ask who else heard it and who else participated. If you hear the same name(s) cropping up again and again when your son has been in trouble, you know you're contending with a group problem. You may try to break up the pack by:

- contacting the parents of his cohorts and gaining their perspectives and cooperation in stopping the harassment
- grounding your son from spending free time with other troublemakers
- asking his teachers to separate them in class
- asking the principal to separate them at lunch and during other activities
- steering your son toward other friends, a positive church youth group, a fascinating hobby . . . or even a job

These measures may not work because the social caste system at school can be ironclad. But at least you are not giving him a green light to head down the road of harassment unheeded.

For both sons and daughters, it is good to involve the school counselor. The best avenue is for the teen to initiate the conference. If, however, the problem is not resolved, you have the parental right to inform the counselor of your concerns.

WHAT COULD YOU SAY?

To Teens Who Have Been the Harasser

Initially teens may fiercely resent your intrusion into their social life. But you need to be up front with them. "Jason, believe me, I am for you no matter what difficulty you're in. I know this is a tough time. And that's why we have to talk. Under no circumstances are you to touch Mary in any way. You are not even to talk or walk with her. Don't joke with her or about her. If someone asks you about what happened, simply reply, 'All I can say is I acted inappropriately and it won't happen again.' [Have Jason repeat each sentence with you.]

"Son, you also need to say those words to Mary and ask her to forgive you. I will try to set up a time through her parents for you to call her or meet with her briefly. I will be right by your side. The Bible says, 'Whoever conceals his transgressions will not prosper, but he who confesses and forsakes them will obtain mercy' (Prov. 28:13).

"I don't want to have to curtail your free time with others, but once you chose to cross a sexual boundary, you chose to suffer the resulting repercussions. For a month you will have no outside activities after school or on weekends.

"I want to be able to trust you again. If you prove yourself trustworthy, you will receive the resulting reward of restored privileges. I believe in you, and I'm counting on you to not let me or yourself down. I do not want to see your life ruined, but engaging in sexual harassment *can do just that*!"

To Teens Who Have Been Harassed

Being sexually harassed is both angering and demeaning. Your son or daughter really needs your help in acknowledging his or her feelings as well as with how to respond appropriately to the harassment. "Honey, what has happened to you is wrong. If at times you wonder, *What did I do to cause this?* just know that no one makes another person behave inappropriately.

"It hurts and angers me that someone would be so degrading to you. I know you may feel enraged and want to crawl into a hole at the same time. Just know your anger is totally justifiable. The Bible says, 'Be angry and do not sin' (Eph. 4:26). Just be sure to release it so you won't be consumed by it. Never feel it's wrong to report sexual harassment. You are on the side of truth, and truth will set you free. Let's pray together for a couple of days about how the Lord wants you to see this situation and how He wants you to handle it. Then we'll talk again and see what the Lord has revealed to each of us. And let's pray for your harasser too. He really needs the Lord in his life."

WISDOM FROM GOD'S WORD

No matter what you and your teens decide to do about the sexual harassment, most important is the attitude of their heart. While it is human nature to respond with anger, it is the Lord's nature to temper it with love. By praying for the unmet need in the harasser's life, your teens are not acting weak; they are doing something strong.

Do not be overcome by evil, but overcome evil with good. (Rom. 12:21)

One of the most graphic Scriptures on sexual sin is found in the book of Proverbs. If your son has been the harasser, pray that this Scripture will continue to burn in his heart:

Can a man scoop fire into his lap without his clothes being burned? (Prov. 6:27 NIV).

Additional related resources (audio and print) are available from Hope for the Heart (http://www.hopefortheheart.org/):

Victimization; Dating

Personal Boundaries

24

Procrastinating

Once again you find yourself in an all-too-familiar situation. You and your family are sitting in the car in the driveway. The engine is running. It is hot. Everyone is grumpy. You are already ten minutes late leaving, but you have to wait for your sixteen-year-old daughter . . . as usual.

You honk the horn for the fourth time. Then everyone in the car perks up when they see her finally appear in the doorway. But it is a false hope that you will be leaving right away because she chirps, "Oops! Forgot my sunglasses!" and disappears back into the house. You have about had it and are now convinced that something has to be done!

Procrastinating is one of those tendencies that seem to be pre-wired in certain kids. You will know early on if you have a procrastinator—you will be reminding her to get up, reminding her to get ready, reminding her to get her things together, and she will still be ten minutes late every time. This tendency is one of those problems made worse by adolescence—when more responsibility is resting on your teen's shoulders to get to places on time.

Perhaps she is responsible for taking younger siblings to school or she has a job for which she must not be late. Gaining control of this habit becomes crucial because when she is driving, she's likely to make up for lost time by going just a little bit faster and taking a few more chances on the road. Accident investigators say the number-one cause of traffic accidents is excessive speed and recklessness.

A newspaper article some time ago told of a young woman who became a paraplegic as the result of her car's colliding with another when she tried to beat the stoplight. She had been in a hurry because she was late. She was quoted as saying something to the effect, "Every time I sleep, I dream about that accident. I relive it over and over again. I can't help it. It always ends the same—the screeching brakes, the horrible crunching, the spinning out of control. If only I had left the house ten minutes earlier, I would not have felt pressed to try to make that light. I am in a wheelchair today because of ten minutes." How do you prevent something like this from happening to your teenager?

WHAT COULD YOU DO?

Growth and maturity in this area come from stepping aside and allowing natural repercussions to occur. The temptation to rescue or enable will only delay your teens' learning to take responsibility. Always ask yourself, *What is the worst thing that can happen if my teen does not meet a deadline?* Growth comes in this area when the negative repercussions of procrastination and the positive rewards of timeliness directly affect them.

Chances are, your teen wants to correct this bad habit as much as you want her to. When she was younger, it may have been a way to put off an uncomfortable situation, assert control, or create excitement, but now her scrambling around to make up for lost time is far more than frustrating. Sit down with her and brainstorm about what she thinks can be done. Look at her schedule to see whether certain times of the day are more troublesome for her. For instance:

- Does she need to get up fifteen minutes earlier in the morning? Or maybe she needs to shower before going to bed.
- Is she trying to do too much at the last minute? See what she can do ahead of time.
- Is she not being realistic about how long the drive takes? If the freeway is bumper-to-bumper every day, maybe she should try another route.

It could be that you've already discussed all of this with no result—she's a piddler. She dawdles until she looks at the clock and shouts, "Oh, no! I have to leave in five minutes or I'll be late!" If this is the case, she has to learn to pace herself. Because she paces herself by the clock, you can help by setting her clock fifteen minutes ahead. Even though she knows it's set ahead, she also knows why. The shock of seeing the advanced time whenever she glances up may short-circuit her tendency to dawdle.

One procrastinator I know well was motivated to "get a move on" when her roommate chose to quit waiting on her to go to various events. The time-conscious roommate got tired of trying to use anger as a motivation. (It didn't work anyway.) She decided to maintain a pleasant disposition. She clearly announced the time an hour ahead of when they needed to leave. Pleasantly (for a change) she called out, "The horse and buggy leave at 9:00." Then again at 8:55, "The carriage leaves in five minutes!" And at 9:00 when Miss Procrastinator wasn't heading for the car, Miss Promptness said, "I'm leaving" and drove away. The first time Miss Procrastinator was left behind, she was stunned. The second time—well, she was ready and waiting. (Miracles can happen . . . with the right motivation.)

If your teenage son procrastinates in getting ready, he probably procrastinates in other areas as well. Long-term school projects are put off until the night before they're due . . . his room hasn't been cleaned in weeks—or months.

The old adage is true: *first we make our habits, and then our habits make us*. Procrastination can become a habit that affects every area of your teen's life and can potentially become a lifetime liability. The good news is that with an investment of twenty-one days, he can form a new good habit to replace the old bad habit. Take time to help your teen form good habits.

Begin with one project at a time in order to avoid overload so he won't be overwhelmed. For example, map out a school project and make a realistic time line using colored note cards or a system that works for him. Check with him each night to determine how things are progressing and to see whether his system is working.

Often teens become procrastinators because they don't know how to break down a project into smaller, more manageable tasks, allowing an appropriate amount of time to complete each segment. Have them recall times when they did not procrastinate and encourage them to reflect on how good it made them feel. Success breeds success!

Patience is the key on your part. As a supportive parent, you may become the needed catalyst to help your teen move from procrastinating to being proactive, thus creating a positive skill for life. The writer of Hebrews says, "Let us consider how we may spur [motivate] one another on toward love and good deeds" (10:24).

WHAT COULD YOU SAY?

"Sean, I see you have a research paper due in four weeks. This is a great opportunity for you to practice planning ahead so you won't have to pull an all-nighter and end up feeling bad about yourself. Sit down and divide the project into phases and then figure out a workable schedule for completing each phase. I'll look over each phase as you complete it. You can post the schedule on the fridge so we'll both know when the phases are due. You'll be rewarded with the peace of mind that comes from having a project ready on time. Ephesians 5:15–16 says, 'Look carefully then how you walk, not as unwise but as wise, making the best use of the time, because the days are evil.' Each moment given to us by God is a precious gift. I want to help you make the very best use of God's gift.

"I'll expect the schedule to be ready by Sunday night. If you don't have it ready by then, no TV until it's finished. And the same is true for each phase. You will be amazed at how good it feels not to be stressed when you turn something in on time. You'll be so pleased with yourself, and you can bet your teacher will stand up and take note. Let me know if you have trouble figuring out how you want to divide the project, and I'll be happy to help you."

WISDOM FROM GOD'S WORD

Habits are never easy to break. Procrastination is certainly no exception. God's Word offers a guiding principle that can help your teenagers realize that doing things late is not the proper behavior from your perspective or from God's.

> There is a time and a way for everything, although man's trouble lies heavy on him. (Eccles. 8:6)

Additional related resources (audio and print) are available from Hope for the Heart (http://www.hopefortheheart.org/):

Procrastination; Time Management

25

Money Troubles

Your son has developed a hole in his pocket or an unquenchable appetite for something. Within a week he has managed to spend his entire monthly allowance. When you approach him about this, he unloads on you. "Dad, if I show up at school wearing those shoes, I'll look stupid!

"And how can I invite anybody over if I don't have the latest music? Nobody will come! And everyone meets at Chuckie's after school for burgers—am I supposed to say, 'Sorry, I can't afford it'? And how am I going to get to know Stephanie if I can't take her anywhere? Come on, Dad!"

Sound familiar? You're thinking, *Kurt, you don't have a clue of what it costs to raise teenagers—auto expenses, school-related expenses, church youth group expenses . . . to name a few.*

Moreover, there is computer equipment, which is rapidly becoming the norm for doing schoolwork or preparing to earn a living. Meanwhile, as you're sacrificing to tuck away money for college, your teens complain that they are social outcasts because of their lack of cash. Not only are you hard-pressed to help, but also you know they want a lot more than they need.

WHAT COULD YOU DO?

One obvious solution may be a part-time job. Many teens work—out of sheer necessity. In some states, young teens can work limited hours in specified fields, such as retail and food services. The problems come when employers start expecting more hours than a part-time student can comfortably work or when their grades start suffering. Also sports, volunteer work, or extracurricular activities, all of which are important to college admissions offices, sometimes preempt the possibility of a part-time job during the week.

Many businesses have such a dire need of regular, reliable help that with a little effort teenagers might be able to locate an employer who will accommodate whatever hours they can work, even if it's only on Saturdays. As a parent, you may have to work Sundays to support your family. However, if your teens work to earn discretionary income, you should insist that they not work on Sunday, and not just because of the biblical admonition (Ex. 20:8–11). Your teens need to join with the family in worshiping together, fellowshiping with other Christian teenagers, and sitting under sound biblical teaching. If an employer pressures your teenagers to work more, work late, or work on Sundays, pursue other options.

Teach your teens to give at least a tenth of whatever income they earn to God's work, as taught by Malachi 3:10: "'Bring the full tithe into the storehouse, that there may be food in my house. And thereby put me to the test,' says the LORD of hosts, 'if I will not open the windows of heaven for you and pour down for you a blessing until there is no more need.'"

Many parents give their teens an allowance in order to provide them with experience in handling money before they are totally on their own. Most parents agree to pay certain expenses, such as clothes, food, and medical bills. Before the school year starts, you both should sit down and agree on each expected expense. Teenagers often take advantage of the summer months to work full-time, if possible, and save part of that income for spending money during the year. However, paying teenagers to do chores they should be doing anyway (for example, making the bed) or paying for good grades is probably not a good idea. They should know there are certain things they're expected to do without remuneration.

Teenagers need to learn to prioritize and economize just as everyone else does who has to work for a living. It is not the end of the world if they can't have everything they want. In fact, it will benefit them. Some repercussions of never going without include never learning to appreciate the value of other people's time and money, never really maturing, and never knowing the apostle Paul's secret of contentment or the joy of seeing God provide.

> Not that I am speaking of being in need, for I have learned in whatever situation I am to be content. I know how to be brought low, and I know how to abound. In any and every circumstance, I have learned the secret of facing plenty and hunger, abundance and need. I can do all things through him who strengthens me. (Phil. 4:11–13)

Take time to establish positive habits with your teens that will last a lifetime. Teach them as well as model the importance of putting 10 percent of your earnings into savings. Show them with actual numbers how a small amount of money can accumulate with interest into a significant amount of savings over a number of years. Sadly, the message of today's world is "spend now—pay later." Study the lives of saintly missionaries such as George Müller or Mother Teresa and see how God rewarded their faithfulness when they lacked resources by providing the financial backing for them to do His work. If teenagers' activities are truly serving Him, He'll provide the means.

By receiving training in the discipline of savings, teens can learn an invaluable life lesson of delayed gratification. Set up an online program, and train your teen how to manage money and watch it grow. The balance of tithing, saving, and prioritizing will set your teens onto a wise life path of good stewardship with money.

WHAT COULD YOU SAY?

To help your teens learn the value of contentment with what they have and how to stretch a buck, you might say, "A very good way to discern what God has for you is through His financial provision. When God wants you to do or to have something, He will provide the means. Let's pray that God will reveal His will for you in this way and that you will trust Him to provide. Realize God's wisdom to us in Hebrews 13:5, 'Keep your lives free from the love of money, and be content with what you have, for [God] has said, "I will never leave you nor forsake you."'

"Let's also set up a weekly budget to help you manage the money He provides so it will go as far as possible. List every expense for each month, when it occurs, and the amount it involves. Then total your expenses and prioritize them.

"Since your expenses might exceed your allowance, make a list of possible ways to earn additional income. Be willing to work. You might need to figure out which expenditures to drop. Ask God to provide extra means if He so chooses, but thank Him for what He does and does not provide.

"Once you have your budget and your plan, pass it by me, and we'll talk about it. If you fail to curtail your spending to match your income, I'll have to step in and do it for you. Realize that God both gives and withholds things for our good."

Again, include your teens in prioritizing. Determine the amount of money available each week, and help them understand the importance of making wise decisions on how they will spend the money. Planning ahead is the key.

Have your teens keep a calendar each month and flag the activities that will cost money. Once the Lord has His portion, allow your teens to make some financial choices, even if they are not always smart choices. You will know when to intervene and provide direction. When the money is not there for some fun activities, they will soon learn to adjust their spending accordingly.

It may be difficult at first, but empower your teens to make choices.

WISDOM FROM GOD'S WORD

One of the most valuable gifts you can give teenagers is to teach them to be content with what they have.

> My God will supply every need of yours according to his riches in glory in Christ Jesus. (Phil. 4:19)

Additional related resources (audio and print) are available from Hope for the Heart (http://www.hopefortheheart.org/):

Financial Freedom

26

Stealing

Your son hurriedly exits your bedroom. Concerned, you walk over to the dresser, open your wallet, and discover that the twenty dollars earmarked for dinner is gone. You feel heartsick as you hear Randy open and then close the front door behind him. You've accepted the possibility that an outsider—a stranger—might rob you, but certainly not an insider—not family. You know he took the money and that this behavior will only get worse without a confrontation.

WHAT COULD YOU DO?

Stealing takes many forms, as illustrated by the following scenarios, all drawn from real life.

In the first scenario, a mother repeatedly had discovered money missing from her purse. Therefore, she carefully counted the money in her wallet, subtly marking every bill. Days later, when she came up short, she confronted her son. She told him how much money was missing and described the marks she had made on the bills. Then she asked him to empty his pockets. She checked his money and showed him the marked bills. Caught red-handed, he admitted he had taken them.

This mother knew her son had deeper problems stemming from his poor relationship with his father. Confronting him with the stolen money gave her the leverage she needed to insist he come to counseling with her. The boy agreed.

Today more and more teens are stealing, not just from their parents and friends, but from stores and places where they eat and hang out.[1] For many, it doesn't seem "wrong" because in their mind, if they want it, they should have it. Therefore, there is no remorse for stealing—only for getting caught.

If your teen has a similar attitude, consider enforcing the biblical punishment for stealing. According to Exodus 22:4, 9, your teenager needs to pay back *double the amount stolen*.

In the second scenario, you find clothing and jewelry items in your daughter's room with security tags still attached. Either a store clerk failed to remove the tags or the items were stolen. First ask the Lord for wisdom. If your daughter is stealing, what is motivating her?

Confront her and listen to what she says. Can she produce receipts for the items? If she claims someone gave them to her, remind her that receiving stolen goods is also a crime. In the spirit of fairness, investigate whatever she says and talk to anyone else she mentions. If your daughter did steal the items, the truth will soon come to light.

I empathize with this situation because I remember, as a youngster, stealing a candy bar from a store. Although I totally denied the theft, when my mother saw the chocolate on my face, she walked me back to the store where I had to confess to the manager and pay for it. (I should have paid back double!) I was so embarrassed. My candy bar caper was a lesson I will never forget.

Today the repercussions of a teen's shoplifting are considerably more complicated. Losses from theft have become so great that many stores automatically report all shoplifting cases to the police, no matter how minor, or even if it's a first offense. Nonetheless, that must not deter you from taking your teen back to the store to return the merchandise. Reporting the theft to the police may be the very repercussion God uses to get a teen's attention. Ecclesiastes 8:11 (NIV) says, "When the sentence for a crime is not quickly carried out, the hearts of the people are filled with schemes to do wrong."

Your teen may be arrested and booked, depending on the value of the items and the disposition of the store manager. If the value is minimal and if it is a first offense, young shoplifters may only receive a ticket and a fine—which they, of course, need to pay themselves. They also may be assigned to probation or a first-offender program, which if satisfactorily completed will allow their criminal record to be expunged when they turn eighteen.

These are frightening repercussions for parents and teens to contemplate, but it is critical that you cover these possible consequences with your teens from the moment they begin to shop. Whatever negative repercussions you would impose will most likely be secondary to the laws already in effect.

Your daughter will need to apologize to the victim. This may even be a condition of probation. An apology makes a difference to the giver and receiver. Make it clear that whenever people steal from a store, they steal from everyone who shops there because theft drives prices up. If an accomplice was involved, that person will be off-limits to your teen.

It's vitally important not to cover up the incident . . . no matter what! Do not rescue your teens from the repercussions of their decisions to shoplift (or you will teach them that they can steal, that they can *sin* with impunity). Proverbs 28:9 (NIV) says, "If anyone turns a deaf ear to the law, even his prayers are detestable."

When the legal conditions have been satisfied, have your teen suggest specific ways to regain your trust so her privileges can be restored and she can experience the rewards that come from making responsible choices. Also plan ways for her to earn money to buy things she will want in the future.

In our third scenario, a mother got into her car one morning and, turning the ignition key, was blasted by offensive heavy-metal music from the car radio. She then noticed the seat was pushed back. Immediately she thought of her six-foot-tall son, who did *not* have his driver's license. Checking the gas gauge, it was a quarter of a tank lower than when she had parked the car the night before.

Her first course of action was to calmly confront the obvious suspect.

If your teens—with or without a license—take your car for nocturnal joy rides, explain that because they've been untrustworthy, they have made it impossible for you to allow them to use the car for a specified period of time until they regain your trust. Emphasize how much you desire restored trust (but still hide the car keys at night!).

In the fourth situation, the law caught up with a teen who was freely downloading music from Internet sites and then sharing it with friends. The music industry sued the fifteen-year-old's family for each song. The daughter feigned innocence stating, "It's not like they warn you or anything that it isn't legal." But she *was* found to be distributing music illegally, a violation of federal law. Ignorance of the law is no excuse, and this family is now "singing the blues" in court.

WHAT COULD YOU SAY?

"Teddy, I know you are excited about driving, and I know it's going to be fun whenever you're able to drive legally, but I'm very hurt and disappointed that you would break the law and betray our trust by sneaking out with the car. If the police had stopped you, the ticket would have cost you several hundred dollars. An accident could have put our entire family in serious financial jeopardy because you are not on our insurance policy, and we could have been sued by anyone you hit. What's more, any of those scenarios would have delayed your getting a driver's license for a very long time.

"I hate that you have done this to yourself, but the car is absolutely off-limits, and due to your poor judgment it's clear you're not ready to handle the responsibility of driving. Consequently, you've left us no choice but to put off getting your license until you can demonstrate the maturity needed for us to trust you behind the wheel of a car. If after six months you have accomplished that, we can revisit the issue of your driver's license. For now I want you to give serious thought to your actions and to their repercussions and to the lessons you can learn from them. In a few days we'll sit down and talk about the insights you've gained. We love you, son, and we have total confidence in your ability to grow from this experience."

In the case of the teen who downloaded music from the Internet, "You know that taking something from someone without paying is stealing. Even if others do it and don't get caught, it doesn't diminish the fact that it is stealing. In our home we do not steal. It's not only a civil law—it's also the law of God—one of the Ten Commandments: 'You shall not steal' (Deut. 5:19). Regretfully, the repercussions of your illegal actions will fall on our entire family. Therefore, you are to devise a plan for making as much restitution as possible over the next three years, and I want you to be prepared to present it before our legal counsel next Monday after school. You will also prepare an apology letter to be given to each recording artist whose music you stole."

As you plan a repercussion for an action, think of one that can produce a change of heart in your teen. Your goal as a parent must be to make decisions that will strengthen a teen's inner moral compass. Jesus emphasized the necessity of being trustworthy even in the littlest things. "One who is faithful in a very little is also faithful in much, and one who is dishonest in a very little is also dishonest in much" (Luke 16:10).

WISDOM FROM GOD'S WORD

God desires to take your teenager from stealing to giving, and He plans to do that through putting your teenager to work.

> He who has been stealing must steal no longer, but must work, doing something useful with his own hands, that he may have something to share with those in need. (Eph. 4:28 NIV)

Additional related resources (audio and print) are available from Hope for the Heart (http://www.hopefortheheart.org/):

Stealing; Ethics & Integrity

27

Gambling

A coworker is having a baby. Everyone at work is putting in a buck for the office pool, predicting the birth date, sex, and weight. Laughing, you pull out a dollar and submit your best guess. You remember actually winning one time and treating the family to dinner. What a hoot!

That evening you're playing a game with your eight-year-old son. He wins and says, "Grrr . . . we should've been playing for money," to which you respond, "What do you mean?" He retorts, "Winning doesn't mean anything unless you get money for it," and he stomps out of the room.

Later that night you and your husband are talking about your eight-year-old's behavior when your teen comes in and abruptly informs you, "I have to have an advance on my allowance, and I have to have it tonight." Your husband responds, "That's the third time in two weeks. I'm sorry, but there are no more advances." Your teen explodes, "I *have* to have it. Don't you two understand anything? I wish I had never been born and for sure not into this stupid family." Then he storms out. You are stunned and perplexed, wondering, *What is happening to our family?*

Most people define gambling as risking money on the outcome of a contest or event. People may bet on things for fun, such as guessing the birth date of a baby or the score for the local Friday night football game. It adds some innocent excitement to the week and is not really considered gambling.

So what's the big deal about teens and gambling?

Most teen gambling is done on the Internet, and for starters, in most states that's illegal. Secondly, the feelings of exhilaration and excitement can be addictive—and teens' brains are primed for addictions. Developmentally, teens function primarily from the emotion center of the brain, and many like to "live on the edge" and thrive on taking risks. The prefrontal cortex, which reasons and foresees danger ahead, isn't fully developed, but their ability to handle technology and play video games is well advanced. They can navigate multiple sites on the Internet with ease. They are accustomed to playing to win and have gained considerable confidence in certain skills that make them a natural for online gambling.

It starts out simple. They play cards with friends, then add poker chips. Then they play for cash and bet on sporting events. Then they purchase raffle tickets, bet on the lottery, and gamble online. Soon everything they do has a price tag attached. Playing a game by itself is no longer intrinsically satisfying. They need the rush of a possible win with a cash prize.

Teens most vulnerable to becoming addicted to gambling are those who:

- experience problems at home
- feel lonely
- suffer from low self-esteem
- want attention and acceptance from peers
- need money
- thrive on the adrenaline of taking chances
- have family members who gamble
- are looking for ways to avoid stress

WHAT COULD YOU DO?

Look for warning signs. Are your teens:

- asking frequently for advances on allowance
- stealing money
- focusing too intently on the scores of sporting events
- using gambling language or terms
- needing to win at any cost
- looking at online gambling sites
- being secretive about actions and activities
- skipping school or making low grades
- developing other addictions like alcohol, drugs, or tobacco
- experiencing excessive anger, frustration, or depression
- showing adverse personality changes

(If five or more of these are true of your teens, help them find professional help.)

Educate yourself on teen gambling, and have resources available to share with your teens.

Research indicates that adolescents are about three times more likely than adults to become problem gamblers. Studies also show adolescents are up to five times more likely to develop gambling-related problems than adults.[1]

While you are evaluating your teens' behavior, evaluate your own behavior as well. A number of studies show that teens are often exposed to gambling through their parents' participation. It may be considered a special time of bonding—visiting casinos, buying lottery tickets as gifts, or placing bets together. Parents need to model what they can realistically expect from their teens. Modeling self-control or moderation in gambling for a teen developmentally lacking in self-control but ripe for forming addictions is not appropriate. Abstinence is the better, more realistic option.

Talk with your teens. As suggested in chapter 14, "Internet Hazards," set boundaries for computer use, and monitor the sites they are accessing. If you discover gaming sites, your teens should be grounded from the computer except for school assignments, which *must* be done in your presence. If they have access to friends' computers, solicit the help of those friends' parents to monitor computer usage. Because of the addictive nature of gambling, the sooner you get this issue under control, the better.

WHAT COULD YOU SAY?

"I know you enjoy the excitement of playing games. I do too. It's important to find things we enjoy. However, I am concerned about your interest in gambling and the problem it is creating in your life and in our relationship. I realize you may think you have it under control, but your actions and the stress you are under say otherwise. I'm open to hearing your thoughts on how we can solve this problem. I want you to find activities you enjoy, but not ones that pose a threat to you.

"Think about what you believe it will take for you to break free of this habit, and we'll discuss it tomorrow evening. I know you want to be rid of all the pressure you've been under, and I am convinced we can conquer this together with the Lord's help.

"If I see that you are making choices that perpetuate your gambling, there will be serious repercussions. They may include reducing your allowance or taking away computer privileges and time with video games.

Likewise, if we see you making responsible choices, we want you to know that we will take you out to dinner and talk about a plan to increase your choices and activities."

This is a great teachable moment to remind your teens that all of our money belongs to God and that we are accountable to him for how we spend *his* money. Once gambling gets in your blood, money will soon become your god. The craving to have more money will soon replace what we know to be true of God's view on money. King Solomon, the richest man in the world, wrote, "Whoever loves money never has money enough" (Eccles. 5:10 NIV).

WISDOM FROM GOD'S WORD

It's a natural temptation for your teens to want money for the things they desire in life. As parents, you need to train your teens in how to earn money in responsible ways. Gambling is deceitful and can be a trap as well as an addiction.

> Those who desire to be rich fall into temptation, into a snare, into many senseless and harmful desires that plunge people into ruin and destruction. For the love of money is a root of all kinds of evils. It is through this craving that some have wandered away from the faith and pierced themselves with many pangs. But as for you, O man of God, flee these things. Pursue righteousness, godliness, faith, love, steadfastness, gentleness. (1 Tim. 6:9–11)

Additional related resources (audio and print) are available from Hope for the Heart (http://www.hopefortheheart.org/):
Habits

28

Conflict over Clothes

You stand at your sixteen-year-old daughter's bedroom door and knock. "Megan, I'm ready to go. If you're going to the mall with me, you have to come now."

Megan promptly opens the door. "Okay. I'm ready."

Your mouth opens, your jaw drops, your eyes widen as you stare at her in disbelief. Megan is wearing a skimpy halter top with no bra, very short cut-off jeans, sandals, and toe rings. You can't imagine her wearing such a getup in the privacy of your own home, much less in public. Megan regards the look on your face and puckers her heavily glossed lips stubbornly, primed for another fight over her use of makeup and choice of clothes. Something must be done, and you know it.

Clothes are more an issue with girls than with boys. Boys generally want their clothes to fit in with the group with which they associate. The more extreme styles are often regulated by the school. Obscene T-shirts, chains, torn clothing, and sagging pants are generally prohibited. Thus the boys' opportunities to shock with their clothing are somewhat limited.

Girls have a different shopping agenda. As they reach adolescence, an important criterion in their selection of clothes is being able to display their physical charms. Thus they will test you (and the school guidelines) with short skirts, short shorts, tube tops, bare midriffs, and plunging necklines. Back-to-school shopping can degenerate into a tug-of-war between a mother bent on decency and a daughter bent on popularity.

Cost, too, becomes an important factor. The most popular clothes can often be the most expensive. Teens may be extremely demeaning about someone else's clothes. Some students feel that not having a closet full of the most desired labels will impair their social status. For this reason, an increasing number of public schools are adopting the private school practice of requiring uniforms. Many teens hate them, but uniforms are a great leveler—no one can make fun of anyone's clothes when everyone is wearing the same thing. Likewise, wearing uniforms can relieve tension in teens (the pressure to fit in by wearing expensive labels is removed).

Where gangs are a problem, uniforms can eliminate the fear of accidentally wearing the colors of a certain gang. Teachers value uniforms because a class with this dress code presents a neat, scholarly appearance and contributes to a sense of order. Principals prefer them because no time has to be wasted on dealing with inappropriately dressed students. Parents love them for the hassle-free shopping and dressing for school.

Although a significant cash outlay may be needed at the beginning of the year, uniforms consistently prove to be a better value than other school clothes. Many schools even have hand-me-down programs from graduating students to those who are incoming.

WHAT COULD YOU DO?

Help your daughter understand the sanctity of her body by sharing Scriptures such as 1 Corinthians 3:16: "Do you not know that you are God's temple and that God's Spirit dwells in you?"

If your teens attend a school where freedom of dress is "sacred," and your expectations about what they will wear differ widely from theirs, study the school's dress code before you ever set foot in a store. It is probably very specific about what is allowed. Administrators are far more strict about adherence to it in September than they are in May.

Armed with the dress code, go through your teens' closets with them to see what they have and what they need. Make a shopping list also of specific items needed for non-school activities. Set a budget. Check the newspaper for sales, brace yourself, and take your teens and go shopping.

If you and your teens are adventurous, it could be fun to give them some cash and turn them loose in a secondhand store. Certain types of vintage clothing are always in vogue and present a wealth of opportunities to be creative and original, not to mention thrifty. Your teenagers may discover that bargain hunting can be fun and that treasures hide in unlikely surroundings.

WHAT COULD YOU SAY?

If Megan presents herself in skimpy, inappropriate attire, you can say, "Megan, many times I've seen you exercise sound judgment, and I respected your decisions, but I can't bear seeing you have so little respect for yourself by dressing like this. Sweetheart, you have no idea how it makes you look. It sends an unspoken message that you want others to be attracted to your body, not your inner person. Positioning yourself as simply an object for lustful pleasure demeans you . . . and the One who created you.

"First Corinthians 8:9 (NLT) says, 'But you must be careful so that your freedom does not cause others with a weaker conscience to stumble.' One of my major concerns is that the way you are dressing right now demonstrates a blatant disregard for the moral character of your male friends. I will assume you don't understand what a snare this is to guys struggling to maintain sexual purity in their minds.

"It's important to both of us that you be respected. Honey, you have ten minutes to change. Hurry, so we can get on the road." (If she balks, say, "Megan, maybe this isn't the best day. Perhaps we can try again next week. I think we'll have a great day together. I look forward to spending time with you shopping for school clothes.")

In the car on the way, you might pleasantly lay out some ground rules. "OK, honey, you know what we need and how much we have to spend. I'm going to let you pick out the clothes. Whatever you find that is on our list and that you can wear to school, I'll put in the cart until we exhaust our budget. Then if you want to put some things back and get other things, we'll do that. I have all day.

"If you find something else you really want and it meets our standards, you can use your own money to buy it. I am limiting my buying this trip to only those things on our list of school needs. Megan, let's make an adult decision now to act with maturity. If there is any arguing or crying, our shopping will stop, and we'll check out with whatever we have. Will you agree to this? Do you think it is fair? Okay. Then when we're finished, let's eat out together. I enjoy being with you—you're really very special to me."

WISDOM FROM GOD'S WORD

Differences in taste within families are to be expected, especially between parents and teens. But if everyone's thoughts toward clothing and makeup are in line with God's thoughts, working with those differences should be a stretching experience, not a stressful one.

> Your beauty should not come from outward adornment, such as braided hair and the wearing of gold jewelry and fine clothes. Instead, it should be that of your inner self, the unfading beauty of a gentle and quiet spirit, which is of great worth in God's sight. (1 Pet. 3:3–4 NIV)

Additional related resources (audio and print) are available from Hope for the Heart (http://www.hopefortheheart.org/):

Self-worth; Identity

29

Bizarre Hairstyles

It's Saturday afternoon, and you're out sweating over the front flowerbeds planting perennials. You glance down the street at a young man swaggering up the sidewalk and shake your head in disbelief. With one quick glance, you see his bright orange hair shaved high on the sides. Feeling sorry for his parents, you hope he's not a close friend of your teenage son. As you look again to see whether you recognize him, the spade drops from your limp hand as the boy walks right up to you with a wicked sparkle in his eye. "Hey, Dad! What's up?" His mouth grins. Your heart groans.

WHAT COULD YOU DO?

You may need to deal with a son a little differently than a daughter, depending on the extremity of the bizarre hairstyles and the underlying need behind them. But the truth is, some people from ages ten to eighty experiment with their hair, constantly changing their look. For teens, the exercise can be valuable as they learn how to manage their hair and decide what looks most flattering on them. Such experimentation is mostly benign. Although it may be disconcerting to see your kids go from brunette to blonde to blue, it's probably best to be tolerant of their experimentation. Part of their identity is finding their own look, and they can't do that if you micromanage their grooming. If your teen is looking to shock or make some political statement, you will want to learn the underlying need driving the behavior and address it.

The reality is, every parent will probably have the opportunity, at some point, to scratch his head over his teenager's choices and wonder, *What on earth is going on here? I want to do what's right, but this is just too much for me.* You need to evaluate what your reaction will be if this happens. Will you major on the majors or major on the minors? That is, in the overall scheme of things, how important is his hair? We often hear the maxim, "Pick your battles." Is this issue really a cause for conflict? Ultimately you cannot have total control over a teenager. The whole point of this phase of life is to prepare your child to live independently of you—to prepare your "kite" for flight. Sometimes that means giving him or her space to learn through experimenting in low-risk arenas, like hair color and style.

Now I can hear you say, "There is no way my teens will get a responsible job looking like this. No one will take them seriously." You may be right, but they'll figure that out for themselves, and they'll decide for themselves which is more important—having money or having a bizarre haircut. I'd vote on the money. But forcing them to change their outward appearance to suit you will not change their hearts and minds, except maybe toward you, and it will likely not be for the better. In terms of guiding principles, you can try to influence them, but you cannot control them.

If you believe this behavior is intended to defy your authority, to hurt you, or to show disrespect for your desires, then the situation warrants a weightier response. As for repercussions, you may present your son with the choice of not going out in public except to school or of shaving off the rest of his hair completely and starting over. In that case, he may resume his social life when his hair has grown sufficiently. As for understanding and resolving the underlying problem of how your teens view and treat you, gentle probing will hopefully reveal their heart issues and open the door for productive healing dialogue. "Pleasant words are a honeycomb, sweet to the soul and healing to the bones" (Prov. 16:24 NIV).

A further option would be for you to keep your teens out of school and homeschool them until their hair grows out. Your teens' school may assist you here, for many schools have dress codes that prohibit extreme hairstyles. If they want to be back in school with their friends, they may have no choice but to tone down the hair and adhere to school rules, just as they do with the dress code.

Many times the scrimmage ends here because all the teen wanted was to see your reaction. The hair-raising stunt may be a clumsy test not only of the boundaries you have set but also of your character: Do you blow up, shout, threaten, and rail over the fact that he used Kool-Aid on his head, coloring that will last only until his hair gets wet? How do you react to outlandish surprises? Is their appearance more important to you than how they feel about you or how you feel about them?

On the other hand you may decide that the situation does not constitute a defiance of authority but is merely a statement of emotional needs. Teenagers are often caught up with the need to belong, to do what their friends are doing. If you think this is the case with your teen, you might shake your head and chuckle as you make a neutral comment like, "Well, that's certainly an interesting look. You've outdone yourself with this one. You definitely won't go unnoticed." Then go back to your flowers. Apart from your comments, chances are your teen will probably experience enough discomfort from the negative looks and comments of others that he will give it up once the novelty wears off.

WHAT COULD YOU SAY?

In talking to your son about it, you could say, "I know you think I am old-fashioned and have no concept of what is 'in.' And I know you want to make your own decisions about your appearance. I'm okay with that as long as you use good judgment and common sense. Tell me, what prompted you to shave off all of your hair? What were you feeling?"

Listen carefully to the answer. It may be, "I was just messing around." That's a common response to anything with which a parent takes issue. So probe deeper: "Well, I hope you don't feel that you have to do something drastic to be noticed and to feel special. You know your mom and I love you just the way you are. We highly value you as the unique person God made you to be. You are our pride and joy. And we have no problem with your experimenting with your hair so long as it is not motivated by your feeling bad about yourself and wanting to change who you are.

"Obviously you want a lot of people staring at you—that's what it will accomplish. I want to ask you something seriously: Do you feel valued for who you are—as a person? Do you feel valued for what you look like? In the core of your heart, do you feel you're really worth something?"

Now you may get an "I dunno" or a blank stare. But there may be a different response if your questions hit close to home. If there was a time in your own life when you struggled with a sense of self-worth, you might disclose it. All young people struggle in this area. Think about a time when you were trying hard to be liked, yet the people you were trying to impress didn't even know you existed. Telling your teens about the experience may help them better understand themselves and identify with you.

Then you could move on to say, "It's taken me a while to learn that a person's real value isn't based on performance or looks or even ability. God created you with an intrinsic value that supersedes all those things, simply because He loves you so much, and I know He is going to do great things with your life."

Now go back to the hair. "I have no desire to stop you from doing harmless things you want to do, but with all my heart I believe that this hairstyle is not going to get you what you really want."

Encourage your teens to take some time and make a list of the positives and negatives of having such a hairstyle. Once accomplished, ask whether there is anything on the list that they can't live with or that they feel would damage their reputation. The key in dealing with teen fads is to lead a discussion that helps the teens check their motives behind their decisions. Thankfully, most fads pass with time without much harm done.

> The wise in heart are called discerning, and pleasant words promote instruction. (Prov. 16:21 NIV)

WISDOM FROM GOD'S WORD

If you want teenagers to view the world and all the people in it with the eyes of the Lord, then model God's compassion before their eyes. Search out the "statement" behind any bizarre look, and remember to check it out before you write it off.

> Man looks on the outward appearance, but the LORD looks on the heart. (1 Sam. 16:7)

Additional related resources (audio and print) are available from Hope for the Heart (http://www.hopefortheheart.org/):
Self-worth; Identity

30

Body Piercing

Your daughter shows up at your office unannounced. "Angie! Hi! This is a pleasant surprise. What brings you around this afternoon?" you ask while glancing uneasily at Angela's friend Gina, whom you don't know well. All you really know about her is that she wears short tank tops, low hip-huggers, and a distracting array of earrings in her ears, one in her lip, and one in her eyebrow.

"Hi, Mom. I just wanted to let you know that Gina is taking me to get a belly ring," your daughter declares. You glance at Gina's navel, which is indeed pierced, then look at your daughter in dismay. Not only has she brought reinforcements in making this request, but she has chosen to make it in front of your coworkers, knowing you wouldn't want to make a scene.

Body piercing is one of the more extreme conflicts you may face regarding your teenager's appearance. Body piercing is more than piercing the earlobes, now considered so benign. Today body piercing may include rings, studs, or pins piercing the lips, tongue, nose, eyebrows, ear cartilage, back of the neck, nipples, navel, genitalia, etc.

WHAT COULD YOU DO?

In regard to body piercing, keep a watchful eye on behavior changes and choice of friends. If teenagers want a certain piercing or come home with one, gently try to find out the reason and how this fits into both their self-esteem and social norms. Respond by discussing rather than reacting with rejection or anger. You can learn more about your teens through listening and keeping the doors of communication open. Pray for the Lord to reveal the true motive behind the body piercing and whether that motive is superficial or significant.

Evaluate the possible reason(s) for body piercing:

- to fit in with peers
- to fulfill a desire for adventure
- to satisfy curiosity
- to engage in creative self-expression
- to rebel against family norms
- to reveal a deep inner need or longing
- to send nonverbal cues about sexual readiness
- to express inner pain in an outer way

Revisiting your own guidelines and boundaries with your teenagers may go a long way toward helping them make healthy, proactive choices physically, emotionally, and socially. Whether they already have a piercing or are contemplating one, your parental role is to do what is in your teens' best interest—not to be manipulated into doing what they want you to do. Saying nothing is not a solution.

Research the issue to become aware of the public health laws in your state. In certain states it is illegal for a minor, under the age of seventeen, to have body piercing without parental consent. (The age is eighteen for tattoos.) Teenagers may have friends who know of shops that will circumvent these laws, but warn them that those places are unregulated by health inspectors and may not follow strict sanitary procedures. A possible infection that results from an unsanitary piercing can literally be life-threatening.

Be aware, many teenagers count on their parents to say no for them. In many cases teenagers don't really want to have the piercing done, but peer pressure seems so overwhelming they don't know how to say no. A firm parental no can actually be a relief. Whether they let you know it or not, your no gets them off the hook and at the same time allows them to save face among their friends. Your teens may be happy to blame you for forbidding something they secretly didn't want anyway.

If other measures fail or you don't wish to be the sole adult voice of dissent, you may want to enlist outside help to provide your teens with enough moral and spiritual support to resist the temptation. Perhaps there's an older sibling whom they respect. Tell the older sibling that you need help. There may be nothing more effective than a respected older brother stepping in and saying, "You want a navel ring? All the guys at college think piercing on a girl is gross. It's a major turn-off." It's amazing what certain esteemed family members can do, whether it's a brother or sister, grandparent, uncle, aunt, or cousin. They can carry much weight within the family dynamic. Proverbs 27:6 (NIV) reminds us, "Wounds from a friend can be trusted."

WHAT COULD YOU SAY?

If your teenager catches you off guard in front of others, you can calmly and quietly say, "Honey, it's always good to see you, but you may not do anything until we have a chance to talk about this. Go on home, and I will see you after I get off work." Then walk away so she cannot argue.

When you ask your daughter why she wants a belly ring, she may tell you that *everybody* is doing it—it's the thing to do." You might counter, "Not *everyone* is doing it. Not *all* teenagers do it because not *all* parents will let them do it."

Say, "I understand how important it is to you to fit in with your friends. But since they obviously like you already, I don't see the need to put holes in your body that ten years from now you will wish weren't there. Later on, when you become an adult, what you do will be your decision. But right now your real friends like you for who you are, not for anything you do to your body. And believe me—sincerely—I like you too! For these reasons I am saying no to your request to do this."

Suggest, "So you won't think I am being totally unreasonable and closed-minded, why don't we each make our own separate list of the pros and cons—the positives and negatives, the rewards and repercussions—of rings and tattoos from our individual perspectives and then get together and discuss what we've come up with. In the meantime, I am trusting you to honor my 'no' to your request."

Guide your teens in a discussion about the qualities of real friends. Proverbs 27:17 says, "Iron sharpens iron, and one man [or teen] sharpens another." Several key points in your discussion about friendship should be:

- A real friend will help you be sharper. Friends help refine you.
- A real friend is committed to helping you do what's best for *you*, not what everyone else is doing.
- A real friend looks at your heart, knows your need to be accepted, and accepts you because of who you are, not because you go along with the "in" crowd.

• A real friend would encourage you to do the right thing (for example, to keep you from being grounded by your parents, if for no other reason!).

Refer to an adult your teenagers like. The example you cite could be your church's youth director, a favorite teacher, or a relative who has been attentive to them: "Look at Dana, who is beautiful inside and out. How could her appearance be improved by a belly ring? Or look at Ms. Anderson, who has her own company. Can you see her fretting over a ring getting caught in her clothes? She doesn't have time." Think about another respected adult (possibly the principal or the pastor). "Do you think having a hole in his nose would be appropriate?" Then ask, "Do you think it's possible that when you become thirty, having a hole in your nose might not be 'in'? Then what do you do?"

Viewing their bodies as a commodity or as a means to gain popularity indicates a serious problem with self-esteem. Examine the reasons *why* your teens want to do this.

Use this opportunity to emphasize the importance of making decisions about their bodies based on what is best for them personally, not on whether they think it will gain them acceptance among their peers. Girls, especially, need support in asserting ownership of their own bodies. For some teens, this is the rationale for piercing: "It's my body, and I can do what I want with it!" In that case you may need to remind them of the fact that "You are not your own, for you were bought with a price. So glorify God in your body" (1 Cor. 6:19–20).

Some would say this is not an issue of right versus wrong and no Scripture expressly forbids it. Others say the Scripture in Leviticus 19:28 forbidding the Israelites from piercing their bodies would be the biblical principle to apply here. However, the cultural issue surrounding this "shall not" involved the pagan belief that certain tribal markings on the body provided supernatural power. The Lord prohibited body piercings under these circumstances because He is the true source of supernatural power—God's people were not to adopt pagan rituals. That is why He said, "You shall not make any cuts on your body for the dead or tattoo yourselves: I am the LORD" (Lev. 19:28). Nevertheless, even in today's culture, body piercings can convey a look that others find offensive. Ultimately, doing what is in the best interest of your teenager is the most loving thing you can do.

WISDOM FROM GOD'S WORD

Being accepted by our peers is important to all of us, but it is especially important to teenagers. Acceptance is often the motivation behind their choices. Likewise, it is often the motivation behind your consternation. Yet, if teenagers can stand alone, not constantly comparing themselves with the crowd, God will produce in them a sense of confidence.

> Each one should test his own actions. Then he can take pride in himself, without comparing himself to somebody else. (Gal. 6:4 NIV)

Additional related resources (audio and print) are available from Hope for the Heart (http://www.hopefortheheart.org/):

Self-worth; Identity

31

Occult Fascination

Your previously well-adjusted teen seems to have morphed into another being overnight. Now Kate wears only black clothes and black makeup. She doesn't go to church anymore, and her grades have plummeted. Not only is she sullen, sarcastic, and secretive, she is also hanging out with an entirely different group . . . all dressed in "Goth." Kate can't abide movies, magazines, or music unless they have dark, disturbing themes. In all candor, the occult holds her captive.

The occult refers to any practice used in an "attempt to gain supernatural knowledge or power apart from the God of the Bible."[1] Astrology, séances, palm reading, witchcraft, goddess worship, and earth religion all promise to divulge *hidden knowledge* to their disciples. In fact, the word *occult* means "hidden." Since curiosity about forbidden things is a human trait, *natural curiosity* is the hook that occultists use to lure unwary teens.

"What is wrong with the occult?" your teens may ask. "Why are you against it?" The number one answer is, "Because God is against it." Make no mistake, involvement in the occult launches you into a realm clearly forbidden by God. In Leviticus 20:6–7 (NIV) the Lord says, "I will set my face against the person who turns to mediums and spiritists to prostitute himself by following them, and I will cut him off from his people. Consecrate yourselves and be holy, because I am the LORD your God."

Wicca is a modern term for ancient witchcraft and is the fastest growing religion among teens today. Teens who practice Wicca can try to justify their behaviors with statements like, "Your truth is not my truth." In other words, they try to make truth *relative*, as opposed to a moral absolute. They mistakenly think they can control their own destiny through different occult practices and rituals. Witchcraft and other avenues of the occult are practiced in opposition to the Bible, which clearly states, "Let no one be found among you . . . who practices divination or sorcery, interprets omens, engages in witchcraft, or casts spells, or who is a medium or spiritist or who consults the dead" (Deut. 18:10–11 NIV).

WHAT COULD YOU DO?

Take time to research why teens become involved in the occult. Actually, people are drawn for a variety of reasons. Some teens feel powerless and want to be a part of a group larger than themselves in order to gain power. Others are bored and crave the excitement and intrigue promised by the occult entertainment world. Still others are sincerely searching for meaning and purpose. In this postmodern world of no moral absolutes, the "whatever" generation simply wants to experience "something." Sadly, some teens go looking in all the wrong places . . . and Wicca is one of those wrong places.

Pray for wisdom in regard to the occult as you educate yourself about occult practices and patterns. For example, consider the choice of clothing. One evening after I taught a large group on the occult, a woman poured out her distress because her daughter began dressing in black—only black. Her disposition had become "dark," her spirit oppressed. This mother went home and *insisted* that her daughter get rid of the *black only* dress style. In fact, this mother had already met with a group of parents who were also concerned about their kids, and they too insisted that their teens give up the Gothic clothes and hard rock.

The result was absolutely fascinating. After a month-long battle over "rights"—as their parents held their ground—the kids switched to country and western music. This mother shared that over a period of time her daughter's countenance literally changed—she was no longer sullen and sad. The other parents along with their teachers witnessed and reported the same change, not just individually but regarding the entire group. The key was the consistency of caring parents who hold to nonnegotiable boundary lines with their kids.

Be aware of warning signs. Take note of any "dark," dramatic changes—black clothing and dark makeup, secretive activities, and sullen friends. Look for tangible items such as the *Book of Shadows*, the Wiccan diary in which teens record their encounters with the spirit world, including the incantations to "make someone love them" or to hurt someone or to cast spells to bring about desired changes. Two other signs of occult involvement include possessing ceremonial knives and/or occult or satanic altars hidden in a basement, closet, or backyard.

Don't be lulled into a false sense of security. Even when a teenager's interest in the occult appears superficial, parents need to take that interest seriously. Dabbling in the occult is dangerous. Casual church attendance is no covering against occult involvement. Even teens who regularly attend church can be at risk. Don't think it couldn't happen to your teens because you have a "good home." The Enemy searches, stalks, and seeks to destroy young people, especially those who would thwart his message.

Discover what is going on with your teenagers—investigate.

Read the lyrics of the songs your teens will hear hundreds of times— typically they're printed on the CD inserts. Lyrics of songs about the occult deal with destruction, distort the truth, and enslave the listener. Therefore, if you find lyrics that reject the goodness of God, corrupt the message of Christ, or exalt the spirit of evil, deal with the situation immediately. Isaiah 7:15 says, "Refuse the evil and choose the good."

Observe what they are doodling. Look inside their school notebooks or book covers for occult symbols or emblems representing anarchy or anti-justice.

Most people are familiar with the backward swastika or the broken cross, but you also should look for any other distorted cross, such as the upside-down cross, the cross of confusion, or the cross of Nero. Watch for the hexagram and the depiction of Diana and Lucifer. Especially be aware of the symbols for Satan, including the inverted pentagram (or Baphomet), the horn-hand, and, of course, the 666 or FFF, the Mark of the Beast.

Contact ministries that deal with the occult or mysticism to learn the significance of the symbols you find. They also will alert you to other clues. Remember that "The truth will set you free" (John 8:32). Seek help from people you know who have a deep understanding of spiritual warfare—perhaps your pastor or another spiritual leader. Ask them to begin waging war on behalf of your teenagers. Be wary, however, of those churches or leaders that do not teach about spiritual warfare—they won't be able to help you. Remember, when you're dealing with the occult, you're dealing directly with the Enemy of our souls.

Personal Boundaries

Initially seek to gain the cooperation of your teens in ridding your home of all objects relating to the occult—CDs, trinkets, games, even items about astrology. Years ago I was given a slender cup with my sign of the zodiac on it—a cup just the perfect size to hold my pens and pencils. When I came into an understanding of the occult, I didn't want to discard the cup, and it became a major internal battle. But then I thought, *If I can't be faithful in the little things, how can God trust me with the big things?* I knew I needed to throw away the cup (not give it away) . . . and finally I did. Only then did I experience the inexpressible peace of God.

If your teenagers do not see the need to get rid of such objects, explain that the mere physical presence of these objects is in opposition to God and gives the Enemy entrance into your home, thus exposing everyone who lives there to demonic influence. Since your home should be dedicated to the Lord who saved you, your admittance of His enemy is an insult to Him.

Acts 19:19 (NIV) states, "A number who had practiced sorcery brought their scrolls [occult materials] together and burned them publicly." To enable your teenager to experience deliverance from the grip of darkness, *you must rid your home of anything related to the occult*, which is directly denounced by the God of the Bible.

Learn to answer the major questions your teenagers might ask. In reality, many people, even Christians, don't know what the Bible says about the occult. For example:

- *"What's wrong with seeking help to communicate with a loved one who has died?"* This practice is not only forbidden by God, but it also opens the door to being defiled by demons. Leviticus 19:31 (NIV) says, "Do not turn to mediums or seek out spiritists, for you will be defiled by them."
- *"What about astrology and horoscopes?"* The Lord Himself gives the answer in Jeremiah 10:2 (NIV): "Do not learn the ways of the nations or be terrified by signs in the sky, though the nations are terrified by them."
- *"What about using magic charms for protection?"* God again gives the answer in Ezekiel 13:20 (NIV): "I am against your magic charms with which you ensnare people like birds and I will tear them from your arms."
- *"What about nature worship?"* The Bible gives the answer in Exodus 20:4–5 (NIV): "You shall not make for yourself an idol in the form of anything in heaven above or on the earth beneath or in the waters below. You shall not bow down to them or worship them."
- *"What about witchcraft?"* The Bible gives the answer in Micah 5:12 (NIV): "I will destroy your witchcraft and you will no longer cast spells."

- *"Why is it wrong to consult the dead on behalf of the living?"* The real problem is that people involved in the occult look to a practice apart from God for supernatural knowledge; ultimately this is a misplaced faith that God absolutely forbids. "When men tell you to consult mediums and spiritists, who whisper and mutter, should not a people inquire of their God? Why consult the dead on behalf of the living?" (Isa. 8:19 NIV).
- *"What about psychics?"* The true test of genuine prophets from God is that they must be 100 percent right, 100 percent of the time, and no psychic is anywhere close to that. Deuteronomy 18:20, 22 (NIV) states, "A prophet who presumes to speak in my name anything I have not commanded him to say, or a prophet who speaks in the name of other gods, must be put to death. . . . If what a prophet proclaims in the name of the LORD does not take place or come true, that is a message the LORD has not spoken. That prophet has spoken presumptuously. Do not be afraid of him."

WHAT COULD YOU SAY?

In talking with teens, take time to connect, engage, and listen. Their eyes may be blind to the truth based on what they've been told. Be gentle and sensitive to their perspective.

Ask, "Do you think astrology is one of the kingpins of the occult? [They will almost certainly answer yes.] I'll admit it's interesting to think that you could get direction for your life from the stars. If I could *prove* that astrological readings aren't valid, would you be willing to study some research with me on the occult?" (Hopefully, they will reply yes.)

Astrology has three major problems:

1. Scientifically, astrology is based on the belief that the sun circles the earth. However, scientists have proven that the earth circles the sun.
2. Sociologically, since astrological readings are based on an exact date and place of birth, identical twins should have an identical future, but they don't!
3. Spiritually, astrology is totally denounced in the Bible. Isaiah 47:13–14 (NIV) states, "All the counsel you have received has only worn you out! Let your astrologers come forward, those stargazers who make predictions month by month, let them save you from what is coming upon you. Surely they are like stubble; the fire will burn them up. They cannot even save themselves from the power of the flame. Here are no coals to warm anyone; here is no fire to sit by."

"I'm really concerned about the interest you have developed in something very dangerous. I love you too much to see you sucked into self-destruction. With all my heart, I want you to experience the joy and peace of a life that is pleasing to God. Let's see what we can do about this together, okay?

"If I see you making choices that are leading you to the darkness of the occult, I will ground you from certain activities and from being with particular people. Likewise, if I see you moving away from these choices, we will open up our home for more social activities for your friends."

Show your teens how to trust in God and in God alone. Investment of time in this discipleship mentoring will be your greatest asset in helping your teens. Everything you say, do, and model regarding God's truths on this subject will impact eternity.

The beloved apostle John wrote, "We know that the Son of God has come and has given us understanding, so that we may know him who is true; and we are in him who is true, in his Son Jesus Christ. He is the true God and eternal life" (1 John 5:20).

WISDOM FROM GOD'S WORD

Curiosity kills more than cats; it kills many teenagers who dabble in the occult not knowing it brings darkness and death. God's Word is clear about the dangers of the occult with its many deceptions.

> Woe to those who call evil good and good evil, who put darkness for light and light for darkness, who put bitter for sweet and sweet for bitter! (Isa. 5:20)

Additional related resources (audio and print) are available from Hope for the Heart (http://www.hopefortheheart.org/):

Occult; Spiritual Warfare; Satan, Demons, & Satanism; Cults

32

Pornography

You go to pick up your son from his first church missions trip and can't wait to hear all about it. Smiling, you turn into the parking lot. Jake and his friends are the last ones to get off the bus . . . but unlike you, they aren't smiling.

The youth pastor looks over at you and at the parents of the remaining boys and asks, "Do you have a few minutes? I need to talk with you." With puzzled expressions on your faces, you follow him into the office. The boys are all staring at their feet, so you know this visit can't be good. You sit down to find out what kind of boyish prank they pulled.

It turns out there was no boyish prank at all. These *stellar* sons, these so-called leaders in their class, shared pornographic pictures on the missions trip with their friends. You get the facts, although the story is written all over the faces of the boys who by now have lost all ability to speak. "Where in the world did you get those disgusting pictures, and what in the world were you thinking? You're grounded . . . *forever*." You confiscate their cell phones, and with heavy hearts each of you heads to your respective homes.

Your mind is swirling. *Where did this start? Was it in Sam's home? His dad seems like the* Playboy *type. Or perhaps Austin's? Is it because he doesn't have his father?* Your head is now throbbing. *Is it somehow because of me?* The guilt rushes in. You feel hurt, disappointed, angry, embarrassed, and afraid for your son's future all at once. Where to turn? What to do?

You send your son to his room with his tail dragging low and tell him you will discuss it later. In your own room you alternate between crying and praying, seeking God's face and wondering what to do. *Is this a one-time event, or is your son hooked on pornography . . . at age thirteen?*

It isn't something *out there* that you need to keep away from your teen—it has now infiltrated your home, and it's simply a click away.

A brief look at the progression of pornographic material over the past half-century reveals an alarming development. In the past, teens were able to acquire porn only through adults, but now they have access to it right from their own computers or cell phones, a fact that's more than frightening. Music videos, popular teenage magazines, and retail store ads that target teens portray pornographic messages of varying degrees. Many of these avenues degrade women as simply sex objects, to be used and abused.

Even with wise parental safeguards in place, teens can be exposed innocently by way of pop-ups on the Internet, pictures in the mall, music heard in a friend's car, and even billboards on the highway. The National Coalition for the Protection of Children and Families states that 80 percent of young people are first exposed to pornography by accident.[1] The appeal to a parent's heart for their teens would be Romans 12:2: "Do not be conformed to this world, but be transformed by the renewal of your mind, that by testing you may discern what is the will of God, what is good and acceptable and perfect."

WHAT COULD YOU DO?

The parents in the opening scenario met together and collectively devised a proactive plan for the boys. Pornography is addicting, and the boys were hooked. A parent who was comfortable talking with the boys about this issue was selected to start a Bible study on the dangers of pornography. The parent also presented God's view on sex: "Can a man scoop fire into his lap without his clothes being burned?" (Prov. 6:27 NIV).

The boys (now men) will tell you God saved them from a lifetime addiction to pornography by allowing them to get caught. Because a loving father taught them God's truth from the Bible, the boys began to realize how enticing and overpowering pornography is. Today these men tell young boys and teenage boys, "You have to decide *every* day that you aren't going to look at pornography on television, in movies, on Internet sites, and in magazines. The desire never goes away. Anyone can become addicted, even people who know the Lord. You have to *predetermine* every day of your life to stay away." Their testimony is a powerful one. The sincere transparency and significance of their message is readily apparent to teens.

As parents, it is your responsibility to raise your teens to be godly men and women. You cannot abdicate that responsibility. Collectively you can combat the culture. In the Bible, the godly man Job set the standard for sexual purity when he said, "I made a covenant with my eyes not to look lustfully at a girl" (Job 31:1 NIV).

- Set boundaries, clearly communicate them to your teens, and explain the reasons *why*.
- Keep the computer in a place in your home that is open and accessible to everyone.
- Make it a policy in your home to know all electronic passwords. This includes passwords for all social networks.
- Install filters and controls—many are available. (See our resource suggestions.)
- Check the sites your teens have visited. The spirit in which you do this is important. If you do it with a spirit of love, you are parenting, guiding, and teaching. If you do it in a legalistic spirit of policing them, you may expect resentment and anger from your teens.
- Realize that pornography's grip is cross-cultural and includes churches. Don't be naive and think that since your teens are in the youth group, they are immune. Girls, as well as boys, are vulnerable to its far-reaching tentacles.
- Be aware that a laptop or cell phone, brought into your house by a friend, could be another avenue to bring porn into your home through Internet access. Inform yourself of other ways your teens can access porn.

Girls, too, can become addicted—for example, to romance novels. The beginning of a book may seem quite innocent, simply a love story, but the Enemy is on the prowl for the hearts, minds, and souls of teenagers. He will stop at nothing. As parents, be aware of what your teens are reading. Certain love stories and books may have titles that seem safe, but they draw teens in and gradually lead them to pornography.

There are few moral boundaries left in our world. The expression "You can't judge a book by its cover" has never been more true. Seemingly innocent covers and titles mask insidious as well as overt messages that lure girls into sexual, lesbian, and even so-called "vampire" relationships.

Parents organizing a book fair for their private Christian school shared this: "It is distressing to think that nothing except the Bible is sacred anymore. Although we requested from the supplier only Christian books, histories, and biographies, we still have a committee of parents and teachers who review each book before the book fair begins. Thank goodness for that screening committee . . . once again, a seemingly innocent title shrouded blatant filth that was designed to lure girls into a lesbian lifestyle, masturbation, and sex before marriage. Written pornography is as overt and insidious as pictorial pornography." First Thessalonians 4:3 says, "This is the will of God, your sanctification: that you abstain from sexual immorality."

WHAT COULD YOU SAY?

Communicate openly with your teens. These difficult issues aren't going away. If anything, they will only grow worse. Boundaries and filters may help, but the most important thing you can do is to use your words to guide your teens into the realization that there are serious repercussions for viewing pornography and sweet rewards for remaining mentally and emotionally pure. "You can't cover teenagers' eyes. You have to teach them to see. Just as you teach them how to drive, you have to teach them about safety, you have to teach them to be critical consumers and that not everything on the Internet is true or appropriate."[2]

"I love you. I care deeply about what you see, hear, and talk about. I care about what images go into your mind, for I know they will affect your heart, mind, and spirit. You may not feel comfortable talking about these things with me at first, but please know I am always here for you. You will hear words, see pictures, hear jokes, and be exposed to things that are contrary to what we want in our family. Anytime you feel uncomfortable with what you see or hear, you have permission to bring it to our attention to talk it through with us until you understand what it means. Then we all will run it through the grid of God's Word."

A parent of now-grown children shares this testimony: "My children brought everything to me. There were times I had to hide the outrage I felt that this level of filth had penetrated the world of my teens. I learned to listen without showing my reaction; otherwise, I knew my teens would quit coming to me. We sorted out fact from fiction—God's truth from the world's lies. I learned that as a parent you have to be forewarned and forearmed. As we talked through these incidents, we grew closer. My young ones learned to trust me and to this day will say, 'Mom, I know I can come to you with anything.' With children of their own, they now seek to cultivate a climate of open communication in which to navigate their families through these cultural wars."

The greatest gift you can give your teens is to be there . . . to walk with them through this maze of immorality. They need you to be present and to be available with your ears to hear their hearts, with your eyes to see their pain, with your hands to hold their hands, with your love to reassure them, with your words to encourage them, and with your faith to uphold them. As you *bond with your teens through boundaries*, you can guide them through this maze unharmed. Galatians 6:7 says, "Do not be deceived: God is not mocked, for whatever one sows, that will he also reap."

WISDOM FROM GOD'S WORD

As you pray that your teens will fill their hearts and minds with the things of God, encourage them to memorize the following verse:

> Whatever is true, whatever is honorable, whatever is just, whatever is pure, whatever is lovely, whatever is commendable, if there is any excellence, if there is anything worthy of praise, think about these things. (Phil. 4:8)

Additional related resources (audio and print) are available from Hope for the Heart (http://www.hopefortheheart.org/):

Sexual Addiction; Integrity; Temptation

33

Drug or Alcohol Abuse

One evening a man flashes a badge in your face, identifies himself as a narcotics detective, and says your son was pointed out as a known user. Surely
this can't be! You've made the boundary line clear to your kids: no tobacco,
drugs, or alcohol. Yet this detective wants to talk to your son Sammy about
his supplier. After an uncooperative "interview" with your son, the detective leaves. Now you're left feeling doubt, defeat, and dejection . . . you're
drowning in a sea of unanswered questions.

Since even in the "best homes" kids succumb to this temptation, your
major goal is to prevent it from happening in the first place. But if it does
happen, you must curtail this behavior before it proves fatal.

Typically, parents begin to see a downward spiral in their child's
personality—a precipitous drop in grades, truancy, and association with
previously unknown "friends." Therefore, parents who see these signs are
absolutely justified in searching rooms and personal belongings. Once the
child is confronted with evidence, strict ground rules must be set in place.
If that fails, an in-house treatment program may be necessary. And if that
fails, the battle for restoration may take years.

Alcohol and tobacco are the gateway drugs for the vast majority of
substance abusers. While they are legal for adults and socially acceptable
(to a degree) for teenagers, they are dangerously seductive and glamor-
ous. Ultimately, underage illegal use tends to lead to adult illegal use with
harder drugs.

DID YOU KNOW?

Fewer teens smoke tobacco today because they are better informed of
the dangers. Kids do listen! That is good news for a number of reasons.
Tobacco contains chemicals that damage the adolescent brain. Teens are

more likely than adults to use tobacco as a springboard to using other, more powerful drugs. Research shows that kids who smoke are at a higher risk for using alcohol and other substances.

Teens get conflicting messages about marijuana. Parents who smoked marijuana as teens need to know it has 500 percent more THC (the active ingredient in marijuana) today than it had when they smoked. THC elevates dopamine levels and can negatively impact the brain's production of dopamine.[1]

> Today's teens who smoke pot are more likely to become addicted to it and to suffer the side effects of short-term memory loss, problems with concentration, and lack of coordination that have always been associated with marijuana.[2]

> Alcohol is the drug that is most likely to hurt an adolescent. . . . The number of adolescents who drink is three times the number who use marijuana. . . . Heavy alcohol use also interferes with the encoding of new memories.[3]

The "drug of choice" for most middle- to upper-class teens is simply to take things from their parents' medicine cabinets. They have "medicine parties" and simply swap and mix medications to create new "highs."

Then they move on to the "designer" drugs, the most popular being MDMA (methylenedioxymethamphetamine), also known as XTC or Ecstasy. This powerful drug "combines the energy that amphetamines give you with the slight hallucinations of LSD. . . . Users experience an abundance of energy and a desire for touching and hugging. . . . One of the involuntary side effects of ecstasy, however, is teeth grinding and biting the lips and tongue."[4]

WHAT COULD YOU DO?

Realize that parental example is your most powerful tool. When a father who smokes tells his son not to smoke, the impact is severely diminished. Dad needs to ask himself, "Is my addiction more important to me than my son? For his sake I *quit.*" You need to be an inspiration.

Likewise, do you have a well-stocked liquor cabinet? Is it accessible to your kids? (Don't imagine that they don't know where you keep the key.) If parents think it's okay to let their kids drink now and then, the law disagrees. For instance, in Texas if you allow underage kids to drink in your home, *you* could be arrested.

Have regular conversations with your teens about what you expect and what repercussions will be enforced if this expectation is not met. An experiment equals one time . . . a second high is no longer an experiment. Establish clear boundaries in this area. Remind your teens that the *reward* for responsible choices is increased freedom, but the *repercussion* for irresponsible choices is decreased freedom. This means, once you know the *actual situation* in which your teens are "using," limit their freedom in those situations. For example:

- If drinking happens only with *certain people*, then cut off contact with those people.
- If the drinking happens only in *certain places*, then stop your teens from going to those places. If you can't do this, then readjust your schedule so that you go with them.

If you don't know the level of your teens' involvement in drugs, then become a detective. Explore the motivation by thoughtfully asking: (1) Was it curiosity? (2) Was it social? (3) Was it peer pressure? Open communication is essential for you to assess the situation and determine what course of action to take.

Your teens need to hear that you unequivocally support the civil laws against drug use. Without bashing them over the head with Scripture, explain the biblical principle of submitting to the governing authorities (1 Pet. 2:13). In critical situations, some parents call the police when their disrespectful teenagers crossed the drug line.

Before your situation becomes critical, calmly and clearly communicate that your teens must respect you regarding illegal substances or you will have to call the police because what they are doing is not only illegal but also is endangering their lives and even the lives of others. This should not be done as a power play—it should be done with a grieving heart. Your teens *should see you agonizing over the decision*. With police involvement, they need to realize that they forced your hand—if they choose the action, they choose the repercussion.

Research the effects of drugs, pray for wisdom as a parent, and pray that the Lord will prepare the hearts of your teenagers to hear the truth about what they are doing to themselves. Then sit down with your teenagers and present your findings.

WHAT COULD YOU SAY?

Make it clear that you can't control their life, but you do want to trust them to make the right choices. You can say, "The best thing you can do for yourself is make choices that will leave the doors of your future open to you. Each negative choice—and this particular one is a doozy—slams a door shut that may never open again, no matter how badly you desire it. Are you content to throw away the dreams you have for your future?"

Teens have a high antenna for honesty and transparency. If they believe you have their best interest at heart and that you are sharing real consequences of what can happen if they drink alcohol or take drugs, they are more likely to hear you.

"I hope you know how much I love you. It hurt me deeply to find out what you've been doing. I disapprove, but mostly I'm scared for you. I know I can't control what you do. Please take a long, hard look at what you're doing to yourself. I'm not saying this to restrict you; I'm saying it to protect you. I know part of the reason you're doing this is because of your friends. I want you to have friends. But I don't think this group is doing themselves or you any good. Perhaps they don't have all the facts. Let's look at this." Then pull out the chart at the end of this chapter that lists the damaging effects of numerous drugs. Talk about it together. Let them ask questions. Ask them key questions also.

"Are you aware of the high cost of tobacco?"

- More than 400,000 Americans die prematurely each year from chronic cigarette use.[5]
- Over $90 billion is spent annually on health-care problems related to smoking.[6]
- Eighty percent of smokers became addicted to nicotine as teenagers.[7]
- About half of teen smokers are also heavy alcohol users.[8]

"Are you aware how marijuana physically damages the body?" It . . .

- destroys brain cells,
- damages short-term memory retention,
- causes lethargy and personality change,
- decreases the attention span and motivation.

In regard to marijuana, tell your teens how "62 percent of adults who used marijuana before the age of fifteen have used cocaine at some point during their lives."[9] Marijuana has more carcinogens than tobacco. It decreases motivation and can reduce reaction time as much as 40 percent, which makes a stoned driver as dangerous as a drunk.[10]

Talk about inhalants. Sniffing glue can impair judgment, causing a loss of self-control that leads to violent behavior. It can cause suffocation and long-term brain damage. It affects the central nervous system and can cause death.

Walk your teens through the effects of cocaine. It is highly addictive, especially in the form of crack. Dr. David Walsh reveals that "Cocaine is physically and psychologically dangerous because it affects three neurotransmitters. . . . [It] also increases serotonin, which can lead to an inflated sense of confidence . . . resulting in greater energy. Together the three neurotransmitters contribute to the infamous cocaine high."[11] This highly dangerous drug disrupts the brain's control of the heart and respiration, causing angina, heart palpitations, arrhythmia, and even death.

One of the most recent causes of teen deaths is experimentation with heroin and the addition of items from parents' medicine cabinets. These can be lethal combinations.

Stimulants or uppers are more accessible to kids because they are sold as appetite suppressants. That doesn't mean they are more safe, however. They can produce tremors, loss of coordination, skin disorders, hallucinations, delusions, paranoia, permanent brain damage—and death due to heart failure or stroke.

Then there are downers—barbiturates and tranquilizers. These can cause respiratory depression, coma, and death, such as was the case with Michael Jackson.

When you have discussed all this information with your teens, place a hand on them and pray for healing, for peace, and for wisdom for both of you as you work together to get them back on the right road and to "hate every wrong path" (Ps. 119:128 NIV).

WISDOM FROM GOD'S WORD

Peer pressure among teenagers is powerful and can be used both constructively and destructively. As you challenge your teenagers to model Christlike character, they can influence others to do the same. Ultimately God holds us all—sons, daughters, parents—responsible for our choices. Remind your teens that they can either cause others to stumble by their compromises or keep others from stumbling by their convictions. Romans 14:21 says, "It is good not to . . . drink wine or do anything that causes your brother to stumble."

God will enable you to stand strong against every temptation and to break every stronghold.

> No temptation has seized you except what is common to man. And God is faithful; he will not let you be tempted beyond what you can bear. But when you are tempted, he will also provide a way out so that you can stand up under it. (1 Cor. 10:13 NIV)

WHAT ARE THE FOUR MAJOR DRUG CLASSIFICATIONS?[12]

Drugs are generally classified into four major groups depending on their effect on the body.

1. Depressants are drugs that produce a calming effect and slow down the central nervous system.

> *Prevalent types are . . .* alcohol, sedatives (sleeping pills), tranquilizers (Valium), barbiturates ("downers" and organic solvents [model airplane glue, gasoline, and aerosols]).
>
> *Psychological symptoms are . . .* poor concentration, distorted thinking, lack of judgment, and aggressiveness.
>
> *Physical effects are . . .* drowsiness, slurred speech, lack of coordination, tremors, decreased energy, coma, impaired vision, decreased pulse rate and blood pressure, respiratory depression, and death.

The Bible refers to those who . . .

> stagger from wine and reel from beer . . . and are befuddled with wine; they reel from beer, they stagger when seeing visions, they stumble when rendering decisions. (Isa. 28:7 NIV)

2. Stimulants are drugs that excite bodily functions and speed up the central nervous system.

> *Prevalent types are* . . . cocaine, crack, meth, and amphetamines ("speed" or "uppers").
>
> *Psychological symptoms are* . . . excitability, increased energy, exaggerated self-confidence, heightened sexual drives, temporary exhilaration, irritability, apprehension, and intensification of all emotions.

Physical effects are . . . hyperactivity, restlessness, insomnia, loss of appetite, dry mouth, bad breath, itchy nose, dilated pupils, rapid and unclear speech, perspiration, headaches, dizziness, elevated blood pressure and heart rate, psychosis, and death.

The book of Proverbs describes those who walk without wisdom, those who are victims of their own folly. Like the one who takes stimulants . . .

Disaster will overtake him in an instant; he will suddenly be destroyed—without remedy. (Prov. 6:15 NIV)

3. Hallucinogens are drugs that alter and distort reality.

Prevalent types are . . . LSD, marijuana, PCP ("angel dust"), and mescaline.
Psychological symptoms are . . . hallucinations, heightened sensitivities, anxiety attacks, lowered inhibitions, and out-of-body experiences.
Physical effects vary with the drug. LSD acts as a stimulant; marijuana acts as a depressant (reactions differ with each individual): sleeplessness, loss of appetite, increased energy, increased pulse rate and blood pressure, eyes fixed in a blank stare or rapid involuntary eye movements, slurred or blocked speech, higher rate of accidents and violence, disorientations and death.

Although the Bible does not directly mention hallucinogens, it does address the hallucinogenic effect of alcohol, which is frightening and disturbing.

Your eyes will see strange sights and your mind imagine confusing things. You will be like one sleeping on the high seas, lying on top of the rigging. "They hit me," you will say, "but I'm not hurt! They beat me, but I don't feel it! When will I wake up so I can find another drink?" (Prov. 23:33–35 NIV)

4. Narcotics are drugs that reduce pain and elevate a person's mood.

Prevalent types are . . . opium, morphine, codeine, heroin, methadone, and meperidine.
Psychological symptoms are . . . temporary euphoria, dulled senses, lethargy, and confusion.
Physical effects are . . . relief of pain, droopy eyelids, constricted pupils, slowed reaction and motor skills, drowsiness, lack of coordination, depressed reflexes, dry mouth, constipation, scars or abscesses at injection sites, and death.

Personal Boundaries

When you are in pain, rather than turning only to drugs, turn to the Lord, be dependent on him, and seek his direction for pain relief.

I am in pain and distress; may your salvation, O God, protect me. (Ps. 69:29 NIV)

FIGURE 33–1

Drug Name	Drug Classification	Desired Effect (how administered)	Dangers	What to Look For
Alcohol (beer, wine, liquor, booze, juice, sauce, brew, vino)	Depressant	Intoxication, sensory alteration, anxiety reduction (swallowed)	Addiction, toxic overdose, toxic psychosis, nausea, headache/hangover, brain, stomach, and liver damage, fetal alcohol syndrome; dependency, blackouts, aggression, depression, withdrawal, accidents due to impaired motor control and judgment, dangerous withdrawl	Smell of alcohol on clothes or breath, relaxation, intoxication, drowsiness, slow reflexes, glazed eyes, uncoordinated movement, slurred speech, confused behavior, excessive sleep
Amphetamines (*Adderall, Biphetamine, Dexedrine, Dextroamphetamine:* black beauties, hearts, LA turnaround, truck drivers, uppers, ups, speed, crank, Strawberry Quick, white crosses, dexies, bennies, crystals, Rx diet pills)	Stimulant	Alertness, energy (injected, swallowed, smoked, snorted)	Addiction, increased heart and blood pressure, elevated metabolism, impulsive behavior, fidgety, strange body odor, licking lips, absences, verbal outbursts, rapid/irregular heartbeat, reduced appetite, weight loss, dry mouth, stomach upset/pain, nausea/vomiting, diarrhea, sleeplessness, dizziness, headache, malnutrition, stroke, delusions, hallucinations, irritability, agitation, aggression, paranoia, toxic psychosis, violence, depression, skin disorders, ulcers, tremors, loss of coordination, anxiety, restlessness, delirium, panic, tolerance, seizures, heart failure, death	Pills, capsules, talkativeness, wakefulness, weakness, slurred speech, loss of sleep and/or appetite, irritability, anxiety, weight loss, hyperactivity

Drug Name	Drug Classification	Desired Effect (how administered)	Dangers	What to Look For
Amyl and Butyl Nitrite (liquid incense, poppers, room odorizer, video head cleaner, leather cleaner, rush, locker room, snappers)	Stimulant, Vasodilator	Exhilaration (inhaled)	Damage to heart and blood vessels, may aggravate heart problems	Sold in small brown bottles labeled as "video head cleaner," "room odorizer," "leather cleaner," or "liquid aroma"
Anabolic or Androgenic Steroids (arnolds, gym candy, pumpers, roids, stackers, weight trainers, juice)	Synthetic hormone	Increased muscle mass and strength (injected, swallowed, applied to skin)	Acne, irritability, aggression, male breast development, cardiovascular disease, stroke, blood clots, liver damage, jaundice, fluid retention, high blood pressure, increased LDL cholesterol, decreased HDL cholesterol, renal failure, trembling	Pills, syringes, needles
Analogs of Synthetic Narcotics (China White, synthetic heroin, MPTP, MPPP, PEPAP, Ecstasy, MDA, MDMA, Eve, MMDA, MDEA, XTC, TMA, STP, PMA, DOB)	Narcotic (opiate) analgesic	Euphoria, exhilaration (injected, smoked, snorted)	Addiction, MPTP-induced Parkinson's Disease (uncontrollable tremors, drooling, impaired speech, paralysis), permanent brain damage, overdose, death	Lethargy (some experience energy rather than lethargy), needle marks, needles, syringes, spoons, pipes, pinpoint pupils, cold and moist skin
Barbiturates (*Amytal, Nembutal, Seconal, Phenobarbital:* downers, bluebirds, barbs, reds, red birds, phennies, tooies, yellows, yellow jackets, blues)	Depressant, sedative hypnotic	Anxiety reduction, euphoria (swallowed, injected)	Severe withdrawal, dependency, possible convulsions, toxic psychosis, birth defects, lowered inhibitions, slowed pulse, lowered blood pressure, poor concentration/fatigue, confusion, impaired coordination/memory/judgment, respiratory depression and arrest, death	Capsules, tablets, needles/syringes

Personal Boundaries

Drug Name	Drug Classification	Desired Effect (how administered)	Dangers	What to Look For
Benzodiazepine Class (Other than flunitrazepam; *Atvian, Xanax, Valium, Librium, Halcion:* candy, downers, sleeping pills, tranks)	Depressant, sedative Rx drugs	Relaxation (swallowed, injected)	Dependence, unusual excitement, euphoria, sedation, drowsiness, hallucinations, memory loss, hypotension, muscle twitching, tremor, aggression, mania, impaired motor function, life-threatening withdrawal, suicidal ideation, coma	Capsules, tablets, needles/syringes, pill bottles
Bupremorphine (suboxone subutex)	Narcotic (opiate analgesic)	Stop opiate withdrawl (sublingual-under the tongue to dissolve)	Addiction, shortness of breath, constipation, headache, insomnia, GI upset, sweating, low blood pressure	Pills, bottles
Cocaine (coke, rock, crack, toot, blow, bump, C, candy, Charlie, snow, pearl flake, girl, doing a line, lady, base, baseball, crank)	Stimulant, local or topical anesthesia	Stimulation, excitation, euphoria (injected, smoked, snorted)	Addiction, malnutrition, depression, violence, convulsions, nasal injury, chest pain, heart attack, seizure, psychosis, stroke, brain or lung damage, dependency, elevated heart rate, increased blood pressure/temperature, restlessness, delirium, panic, aggression, paranoia, death	Glass vials, glass pipe, white crystalline powder, crystalline rocks, razor blades, syringes, spoons, needle marks, straws, mirrors, rolled bills
Cocaine freebase (base, freebase, crack, rock, C, dynamite, snorting)	Stimulant, local or topical anesthesia	Shorter and more intense cocaine effects	Weight loss, depression, agitation, hypertension, hallucinations, psychosis, chronic cough, tremors	Glass vials, glass pipe, crystalline rocks, razor blades, syringes, spoons, needle marks
Codeine (*Empirin with Codeine, Fiorinal with Codeine, Robitussin A-C, Tylenol with Codeine:* Captain Cody, schoolboy; with *glutehimide:* doors & fours, loads, pancakes and syrup)	Narcotic (opiate) analgesic	Euphoria (injected, swallowed)	Addiction, constipation, loss of appetite, nausea, organ damage, overdose, death	Liquid cough syrup with codeine, pills, syringes, needle marks

Drug Name	Drug Classification	Desired Effect (how adminis-tered)	Dangers	What to Look For
Dextromethor-phan (Found in some cough and cold medicines, such as *Robitussin Coricidin:* DXM, CCC, Triple C, Skittles, Robo, Poor Man's PCP)	Hallucinogen (high doses of over-the-counter antitussive cold medicines)	Heightened perceptual aware-ness, altered time perception, visual hallucinations (swallowed)	Hyperexcitability, dissociative effects, distorted visual perceptions to complete dis-sociative effects, lethargy, slurred speech, sweating, hypertension, increased blood pressure, liver damage, central nervous system toxicity, cardio-vascular toxicity, sudden death	Liquid, pills, or capsule cough/cold medicine
Fentanyl / Fentanyl Analogs (*Actiq, Duragesic, Sublimaze:* Apache, China girl, China white, dance fever, friend, goodfella, jackpot, murder 8, TNT, Tango and Cash)	Narcotic	Euphoria (injected, smoked, snorted)	Addiction, weight loss, constipation, loss of appetite, heart disease, congested lungs, abortion, birth defects, staggering gait, contamina-tion from unsterile needles (hepatitis, AIDS), overdose, death	Tablet cancer pain medication, syringes, needle marks
Flunitrazepam (*Rohypnol:* forget-me pill, Mexican Valium, R2, Roche, roof-ies, roofinol, rope, rophies, date rape drug)	Depressant	Memory loss, (swallowed, snorted)	Visual and gastro-intestinal distur-bances, urinary retention, black-outs, disorienta-tion, vulnerable to sexual assault, memory loss during time under drug's effects, death	Small white tablet, can be crushed and snorted
GHB (*Gamma-hydroxybutyrate:* Liquid Ecstasy, Liquid X, Georgia Home Boy, Grievous Body Harm, G, date rape drug, scoop, goop, soap, Easy Lay)	Depressant	Euphoria, intoxica-tion, (swallowed)	Drowsiness, diz-ziness, nausea, amnesia, visual hallucination, reduced blood pressure, decreased heart rate, convulsions, severe respiratory depression, loss of consciousness, loss of reflexes, coma, and death; withdrawal: insomnia, tremors, anxiety, sweating, seizures, danger-ous withdrawl	Tablet, capsule, white powder can be mixed with flavored drinks or alcohol

Personal Boundaries

Drug Name	Drug Classification	Desired Effect (how administered)	Dangers	What to Look For
Heroin (H, cheese, junk, dope, smack, black tar, harry, horse, brown, brown sugar)	Narcotic (opiate) analgesic	Euphoria (injected, smoked, snorted)	Addiction, weight loss, constipation, loss of appetite, heart disease, congested lungs, abortion, birth defects, staggering gait, contamination from unsterile needles (hepatitis, AIDS), overdose, death	Powder or brownish black tar substance, pipe, syringes, spoons, needle marks; "cheese" heroin mixture of heroin and Tylenol PM
Inhalants (paint, paint thinner, solvents, gasoline, glue, gases, transmission fluid, correction fluid, hair or deodorant aerosols, fabric protector sprays, vegetable oil sprays, laughing gas, poppers, snappers, whipped cream aerosols or dispensers, "whippets," "huffing")	Stimulant	Intoxication (inhaled)	Suffocation, nausea, vomiting, damage to brain and central nervous system, dizziness, wheezing, lack of coordination, loss of appetite, intoxication, irritability, hearing loss, depression, unconsciousness, cramps, muscle weakness, damage to cardiovascular and nervous systems, dependency, heart failure, sudden death	Chemical odor on breath/ cans/paper or plastic bags/ clothing, paint stains on face/ hands/clothes, redness/sores/ rashes around nose/mouth, intoxication, slurred speech, drowsiness, poor muscle control, red/runny nose, flushed skin
Ketamine (Special K, Vitamin K, New Ecstasy, Ketalar, Ketaject, Super K, Kit Kat, cat Valium)	Depressant, dissociative anesthetic, hallucinogenic	Sensory alteration, relaxation (injected, snorted, smoked)	Delirium, amnesia, nausea, vomiting, impaired motor function, high blood pressure, racing heart, depression, flashbacks, respiratory problems, paranoia, unconsciousness, death	White powder or liquid injectable, syringes, spoons, needle marks
LSD (*lysergic acid diethylamide:* acid, LSD-25, blotter acid, boomers, cubes, microdot, yellow sunshines, "windowpane" pictures on paper, mellow yellow)	Hallucinogen	Insight, distortion of senses, exhilaration, mystical/ religious experience (swallowed, absorbed through mouth tissues)	Intensifies existing psychosis, panic, confusion, suspiciousness, flashbacks, possible brain damage, strong psychological reaction, impaired judgment, persistent mental disorders	Capsules, tablets, micro-dots, paper blotter squares, unpredictable behavior, emotional instability, violent behavior

Drug Name	Drug Classification	Desired Effect (how administered)	Dangers	What to Look For
Marijuana (cannabis—concentrated resin called hash or hashish [boom, chronic, gangster, oil, hemp]) (pot, grass, dope, weed, homegrown, skunk, sinsemilla, Maui-wowie, reefer, J, Thai sticks, joint, blunt, herb, roaches, indica, smoke, mary jane, bugs, bag, dime, quarter, ganja, Acapulco Gold, THC)	Depressant, hallucinogen	Euphoria, relaxation, increased sensory perception (swallowed, smoked)	Cancer, bronchitis, conjunctivitis, birth defects, brain cell destruction, gateway to other drugs, immune system damage, severely strains cardiovascular system, frequent respiratory infection, alters mood, inhibits motivation, impairs short-term memory, hampers concentration, dependency, altered perception, anxiety, slowed thinking/reactions, addiction	Rolling papers, cigar wrappers, pipes, water bong, green or gray dried plant material, seeds, plastic bags, odor of burnt hemp rope, roach clips, dry mouth, hunger, reduced concentration or coordination, laughing, hunger
MDA, MDE, MDMA, MMDA (*methylenedioxymethamphetamine*: love drug, E, ecstasy, STC, X, Adam, clarity, Eve, Lover's speed, peace, STP, Hug, Go, hug drug, beans)	Hallucinogen (amphetamine based neurotoxin)	Same as LSD (swallowed, injected, snorted, or used as a suppository)	Neurotoxic, same as LSD, time distortion, sense of distance and estrangement, anxiety, catatonic syndrome, paranoia, brain damage, confusion, depression, psychotic episodes; physical effects can last weeks, increased heart rate and blood pressure, acne-like rash, liver damage, loss of appetite, fatigue	Produced illegally – variety of pills with different logos stamped on tablets
Mescaline (peyote cactus) (mesc, peyote, peyote buttons, cactus)	Hallucinogen (milder than LSD)	Same as LSD (swallowed, smoked)	Same as LSD, and extreme mood swings, distortion of senses and perceptions, deep depression	Disk-shaped buttons chewed, soaked in water and drunk or ground into powder and placed in a capsule
Methadone (dolly)	Narcotic (opiate) analgesic	Euphoria, opiate withdrawal prevention (swallowed), effective for chronic pain	Addiction, constipation, loss of appetite, nausea, increased sleep apnea, respiratory suppression, organ damage, overdose, sudden cardiac arrest, death	Dispensable diskettes (usually white or cherry colored), tablets

Personal Boundaries

Drug Name	Drug Classification	Desired Effect (how administered)	Dangers	What to Look For
Methamphetamine (*Desoxyn:* crystal, crystal meth, chalk, crank, fire, glass, go fast, ice, meth, tweak, speed, dope, raw, Strawberry Quick)	Stimulant	Euphoria, alertness, loss of appetite (injected, swallowed, smoked, snorted)	Irritability due to sleeplessness, illness due to weakening of the immune system, tooth loss, sexual compulsion, seizures, stroke, narcolepsy, hyperthermia, cardiac toxicity, renal failure, liver toxicity	Tablets, powder, crystalline rocks, syringes, spoons, needle marks; meth mixed with strawberry flavoring to mask acidic taste; pseudoephedrine cold medicine and household products used to illegally produce methamphetamine
Methaqualone (*Quaalude, Sopor, Parest:* ludes, 714S, mandrex, quad, quay, sopors, blue/red devils, yellows, candy, rainbows, Q's, downs)	Depressant, sedative hypnotic	Euphoria, aphrodisiac (injected, swallowed)	Coma, convulsions, insomnia, dependency, severe anxiety, increased sleep apnea, respiratory suppression, sudden cardiac arrest	Capsules, tablets, needles/syringes
Methylphenidate (*Ritalin, Concerta, Metadate, Methylin, Focalin*—treatment for ADHD: Jif, MPH, R-ball, Skippy, the smart drug, vitamin R)	Stimulant	Euphoria, alertness, loss of appetite (injected, swallowed, snorted)	Dependency, chest pain, heart attack, seizure, stroke, brain or lung damage, elevated heart rate, increased blood pressure/temperature, restlessness, delirium, panic, aggression, paranoia, death	Capsules, tablets, needles/syringes
Morphine (*Roxanol, Duramorph:* Miss Emma, monkey, white stuff, M, morf)	Narcotic (opiate) analgesic	Euphoria (injected, swallowed, smoked)	Addiction, constipation, loss of appetite, nausea, organ damage, overdose, death	Capsules, tablets, liquid, needles/syringes
Nitrous Oxide (laughing gas gases, whippits, nitrous, blue bottle, hippy crack, cartridges)	Depressant, inhalation anesthetic	Euphoria, relaxation (inhaled)	Kidney or liver damage, peripheral neuropathy, spontaneous abortion, violence, nausea, vomiting	Gas canister, balloon with valve
Nonprescription Stimulants (speed, ups, uppers)	Stimulant, appetite suppressant, decongestant	Alertness, energy, weight loss (injected, swallowed)	Same as amphetamines plus hypertension, heart problems, anxiety, headaches, increased blood pressure, fatigue leading to exhaustion	Capsules, tablets, needles/syringes

Drug or Alcohol Abuse

Drug Name	Drug Classification	Desired Effect (how administered)	Dangers	What to Look For
Opium (*laudanum, paregoric:* big O, black stuff, block, gum, hop)	Narcotic (opiate)	Euphoria (swallowed, smoked)	Addiction, constipation, dizziness, fainting, lethargy, nausea, vomiting, anxiety, euphoria, drowsiness, insensitivity to pain, confusion, severe allergic reaction (rash, hives, swelling), difficulty urinating, pupil constriction, watery eyes, runny nose, fast or slow heartbeat, seizures, tremor, respiratory arrest, overdose, death	Liquid, tablets, pipe
Opoid Class (*OxyContin, Lortab, Oxycodone HCL, Vicodin, Percocet, Percodan, hydrocodone:* vike, Watson-387, O.C., killer)	Narcotic analgesic (prescription pain killers)	Relaxation (swallowed, snorted, injected), some use for energy	Addiction, lethargy, nausea, vomiting, anxiety, euphoria, drowsiness, insensitivity to pain, hypotension, watery eyes, runny nose, respiratory arrest, overdose, death	Capsules, tablets, needles/syringes, pupil constriction, (except Demerol, which dialates pupils)
PCP (Crystal, tea, THC, angel dust, hog, peace pill, rocket fuel)	Hallucinogen, dissociative anesthetic	Distortion of senses, stimulant (injected, swallowed, smoked)	Psychotic behavior, violence, coma, detachment, shallow breathing, numbness, nausea/vomiting, blurred vision, drooling, loss of balance, dizziness, terror, psychosis, convulsions, impaired judgment, dependency, confusion, seizures, excessive salivation, schizophrenic behavior, paranoia	White crystalline powder in metal foil or can be mixed in liquid, made into tablet or capsule form
Psilocybin (magic mushrooms, shrooms, purple passion)	Hallucinogen (milder than LSD)	Same as LSD (swallowed)	Same as LSD, and sleeplessness, tremors, heart and lung failure, nervousness, paranoia, flashbacks	Eaten raw, dried, cooked in food, or stewed in tea

Personal Boundaries

Drug Name	Drug Classification	Desired Effect (how administered)	Dangers	What to Look For
Tobacco / Nicotine (cigarettes, cigars, cigarillos, cigs, smokes, butts, cancer sticks, chew, chaw, coffin nails, puff, snuff, spit tobacco, bidis)	Stimulant, toxin	Relaxation (smoked, snuffed in mouth)	Loss of appetite, addiction, cancer [lung, jaw, mouth], birth defects, chronic lung disease, cardio-vascular disease, increased blood pressure and heart rate, stroke, second-hand smoke, death	Cigarettes, cigars, cigarillos, rolling papers, loose tobacco, snuff, chew, spittoon

*For further information on drugs see U.S. Drug Enforcement Administration, Drug Information, Washington, DC: DEA, n.d., http://www.justice.gov/dea/concern/concern.html and National Institute on Drug Abuse, Commonly Abused Drugs, Washington, DC: NIDA, n.d., http://www.drugabuse.gov/

Additional related resources (audio and print) are available from Hope for the Heart (http://www.hopefortheheart.org/):

Alcohol & Drug Abuse; Victimization; Depression; Temptation; Anger; Fear; Self-worth; How to Handle Your Emotions; Seeing Yourself Through God's Eyes

SECTION V
Social Boundaries

34

Gossip

Your teen is on her cell phone in the den, and you can't help but hear parts of the conversation. You keep hearing the name of her best friend, but it is used in a disparaging way. Later another friend calls, and the name of your daughter's friend comes up again, and still not in a positive way.

Then the texting begins and goes on for most of the day. Finally you ask to see her phone. Reluctantly she gives it to you. In the quietness of your bedroom, you read the trail of caustic, cutting words of betrayal toward a girl you thought was your daughter's *best* friend. After praying, you call your daughter into your room.

As Christians we don't always follow the words of Jesus: "If your brother sins against you, go and show him his fault, just between the two of you. If he listens to you, you have won your brother over" (Matt. 18:15 NIV).

If we would take our concerns to each other directly and speak the truth in love, we would have fewer "people" issues. Fear of confrontation or hurting someone's feelings is not an acceptable reason for violating the Matthew 18 principle. While we need to be sensitive to others' feelings, we should understand that hurt feelings are more likely to occur when we talk to someone else about a person rather than talking directly to that person. Instead, in the name of being "nice" and not wanting to hurt people's feelings, we don't say what we really feel and inadvertently cause greater hurt. The Bible tells us to "speak the truth in love" (Eph. 4:15).

Girls are vulnerable to the sin of gossip because of their propensity to use words to communicate. They talk, share their feelings, and use words to connect with one another. These words can be caring and constructive and can be used to build bridges between them, or they can be cold, critical, and condescending, resulting in ruined relationships.

When confronted, "Girls will almost always blame their behavior on something or someone else. Let's say your daughter is accused of spreading a rumor. Instead of admitting her guilt, she'll demand to know who exposed her as the information source, as if the snitch were the person who's really at fault, conveniently forgetting that she was the one who gossiped."[1] Those working with teen girls find that gossip and conflict resolution are generally the main sources of frustration. Once a caring adult or parent establishes a relationship with a teenage girl, she will usually admit to gossiping, to fearing what other girls are saying, and to wanting to stop but also not knowing how to break the habit.

On the positive side, with a strong support group and methodical mentoring, girls learn to hold one another accountable. If they are to be motivated to change, they will need proactive strategies and caring people to help them in the process. As a parent, you can be one of those privileged people.

When girls take the chitchat and nosy chatter up a notch and add a spirit of meanness to it, they become cyber-bullies. A cyber-bully is one who uses electronic media (e-mail, social networks, texting, IM-ing, chat rooms, and cell phones) to gossip. She is both malicious and capricious.

She's the *"Queen of Mean."*

WHAT COULD YOU DO?

Train your teens to:

- examine their own hearts before attempting to solve a problem
- demonstrate the attitude of Christ when they approach people
- check their motives before engaging in a conversation
- build trust in relationships by speaking sensitively, honestly, and lovingly to people
- learn that restoration of relationships and resolution of problems must be our true heart's desire when following the Matthew 18 principle

If your daughter is the *object of gossip*:

- Listen carefully to what she says. If she expresses embarrassment and humiliation over the gossip that's being said about her, do not overreact by going after the *gossipers* yourself. Such an action would only undermine your daughter in the eyes of her attackers.
- Likewise, don't minimize what she is feeling with statements like "Don't worry about it, you're blowing it out of proportion—I'm sure it's no big deal." To her, it is a *very* big deal!

- Lovingly find the middle. Reflect her feelings, and help her sort them out. "I can see this really hurt you. I am so sorry, honey. I find you to be a very lovely and trustworthy person. I believe in you, and I'm here for you." Your words show that you hear her pain and contradict the gossip.

If your daughter is the *perpetrator of gossip*:

- Make it very clear that her behavior is completely unacceptable.
- Talk with your teen about the power of words. Then together take time to look up the following passages on gossip and the tongue, discuss them, and have your teen write them out, listing the instructions (boundaries), the negatives (repercussions), and the positives (rewards) mentioned in each passage: Prov. 16:28; Prov. 26:20–22; 2 Tim. 2:16; Ps. 17:3; Ps. 141:3; Prov. 12:18; Eph. 4:29. Searching God's Word about gossip will help your teen see that the Lord wants us to treat each other with love, respect, and truth. It will also show the value of seeing what God says about other topics.
- Pray that she will have a change of heart, that she will be convicted of the hurt she has caused (repentance).
- Have her go to the girl(s) *about whom* she has gossiped and ask forgiveness (resolution).
- Have her go to the girls she gossiped *to* and confess that she gossiped, ask forgiveness, and set the record straight (restitution).
- If your daughter's heart is hardened to the power of her cutting words, read some of her messages back to her. The goal is to help her hear the power of her words in order to change her heart. If necessary, reread the messages, replacing the girl's name with her name as though they were said of her. The book of Proverbs speaks strongly of the power of our words—"the power of life and death" (Prov. 18:21 NIV).

WHAT COULD YOU SAY?

Go to your teen privately and say, "It sounds like you are having some serious frustrations with Carla. Have you talked with her about this?" Your teen may respond that she doesn't want to hurt Carla's feelings. At this point explain, "It is hurtful to friends to speak about them behind their backs, far more hurtful than to talk with them in person. In this instance it would be better if you talk face-to-face with Carla about what is bothering you."

Say to your teen:

- "Try not to go to Carla in anger. Pray first, then choose your words carefully. The goal is not to hurt your friend.
- "When you speak, use 'I' statements. Rather than attacking Carla by telling her, '*You* hurt me' and putting her on the defensive, say to Carla, '*I*

was hurt when you said . . . *I* was angry because of. . . .' You want Carla to hear by the sadness in your voice that something is not right between the two of you.

- "Find a way to resolve the problem that works for both of you. Then confess to Carla that you shared your hurt feelings with others and ask her to forgive you.
- "Pray with Carla, and ask God to restore the sweet friendship the two of you have had.
- "Finally, you will need to go to the friends you talked to about Carla and tell them you were wrong to badmouth Carla to them and ask their forgiveness. You will find that they will trust and respect you a lot more afterward."

To make it easier for your teen to remember, encourage her to use the "Sandwich Technique" outlined in chapter 3:

- "Begin with the 'Bread of Appreciation': 'Carla, I value your friendship and enjoy being with you.'
- "Add the 'Meat of the Matter' and state the problem. Start your sentence with 'I': 'And because I love you, I need you to know that I was hurt when you . . . '
- "Finish with the 'Bread of Encouragement' and a plan for resolving any future differences: 'When we're upset with each other, let's promise we'll go to each other rather than to other people and gossip about each other.'
- "If you choose to hurt someone through your words—whether they are on paper, texted, voiced, or communicated in *any* way, there will be serious *repercussions*. You will be grounded from using your cell phone or computer or spending time with friends. On the other hand, if we see that you are seeking to be a friend, to work out differences as a friend in Christ, and to use your words to encourage others, we will expand your privileges."

WISDOM FROM GOD'S WORD

We have all been hurt by careless words, and we must be careful not to hurt others with our own words. The Bible is very clear about the incredible power of the tongue and the damage it can do when we violate the boundaries God has established for how we are to use it.

Communication is never 100 percent accurate; therefore, we must not draw conclusions based on secondhand information regardless of the reliability of the source. Most problems can be handled at this level without bringing in a third person. The power of both healing and hurting lies in the tongue; therefore, we must be wise with our words. We must remember that God holds us accountable for every word that comes out of our mouths.

> The tongue that brings healing is a tree of life, but a deceitful tongue crushes the spirit. (Prov. 15:4 NIV)

Additional related resources (audio and print) are available from Hope for the Heart (http://www.hopefortheheart.org/):

Communication; Envy & Jealousy

35
Lying

One Saturday you answer the phone and hear, "Hello, this is Laura's mother. Am I speaking with Claire's mom? I've been talking with my daughter, and I'm afraid that when your daughter told you she spent the night here with Laura, that wasn't true. Laura had told me she was spending the night at *your* house! Actually, what I found out was they both went to a keg party at Chad's house when his parents were out of town."

After thanking her for calling, you hang up in shock, but deep down you're not really surprised. You have come to realize that your daughter has been untruthful on numerous occasions regarding her whereabouts or actions. By this time you feel you cannot believe anything she tells you. You find yourself depressed, angry, and deeply worried.

Lying is the most fundamental of wrongs in that it strikes at the heart of any relationship. No other disobedience can be carried out without a covering lie. No teen is going to say, "Hey, Mom, I'm going to a keg party at Chad's while his parents are gone. I don't know when I'll be home."

Parents dread the discovery of lying (usually there is a pattern, as lies rarely come singly) because they want to believe their teenagers simply would not lie to them. In fact, you should give your teens the benefit of the doubt . . . until the evidence shows otherwise. If you start seeing inconsistencies, you must not look away. Start digging (as painful as it may be) to discover dishonesty and uncover truth.

WHAT COULD YOU DO?

First, be glad you found out. Some parents never figure out what is going on under their noses, rendering themselves useless to guide or protect. The mother of one eighteen-year-old commented, "I am grateful to have such a good relationship with my daughter that she confides in me. However, she also talks to me about what some of her friends are doing behind their parents' backs. These kids get away with everything because their parents never question them or check up on them. It's hard to know what to say when I see the parents."

In this case there's little you can say without betraying your teen's confidences. Besides, if those parents overlook the evidence right in front of their faces, it's not likely they'll listen to you.

I know other parents who pray that their teens *will* get caught whenever they lie or do anything they should not do. The point is not to be hard on them but to protect them from the delusion that they can get away with doing wrong and suffer no consequences. An old adage is true: "Plant a thought, reap an action . . . plant an action, reap a habit . . . plant a habit, reap a character . . . plant a character, reap a destiny."

There are patterns of lying that are difficult to figure out, such as lying about little, inconsequential things. If this is happening, find out what purpose is being served by lying. When I was a teenager, I lied a great deal. I'm not proud of that, but it helps me understand how someone can get caught in that trap. For a while I did not feel guilty about it. It was a part of my life well into my thirties . . . until I finally got to the root of my compulsion to lie.

I remember sitting in my car one night thinking about this. I really wanted to change, but I had no concept of why I was being untruthful. As I thought about my earliest recollections of lying, I realized that my lies always involved protecting my mother. I lied to try to create "peace" in our home. Out of loyalty to loved ones, I lied and did not have a guilty conscience about it for years.

Only after becoming a Christian did I see that one characteristic of Christ is truth. Jesus not only told the truth, He was Truth incarnate. Therefore, I needed to honor the truth and accept the consequences that might come from speaking the truth. Most helpful to me was repeatedly praying this prayer: "Lord, may I see sin as You see it. May I hate sin as You hate it."

Proverbs 6:16–18 (NIV) doesn't mince words in telling us seven things that are *detestable* to the Lord. "A lying tongue" is one of them.

In most homes there is an authority figure who has the right to set the rules. Unfortunately, that rightful authority may turn into a demanding dictator. But even in a benevolent dictatorship teens can feel a sense of powerlessness. That's where manipulation comes in.

Manipulation is a tool often used by a weaker person seeking to control a stronger person by deception. An integral part of manipulation is lying. When parents encounter evidence of pervasive lying, they need to examine whether their system of rules leaves their teenagers feeling so powerless that lying is an attempt to exert some measure of control or independence. If this is the case, parents might consider empowering their teens with more choices—but only after the necessary repercussions have established that lying is not the best way to get what is wanted.

Some teens lie to protect themselves from suffering undesirable consequences for unapproved or questionable activities, as in the keg party caper. Other teens try to do things without the knowledge of their parents in an attempt to become separate individuals. Still another reason people lie is rooted in their need for significance. In this case a student would claim to have made better grades than he actually did or boast of certain athletic or macho feats that he didn't do.

When you have ascertained what you believe is the real reason for your teen's pattern of lying, do some self-evaluation.

- Are your teenagers fearful of you?
- Are you being too strict or overly rigid?
- Are you uncompromising, unreasonable, or unapproachable?

(Consult a wise, objective observer who knows both you and your teenagers in order to get an unbiased opinion.)

When you are prepared to talk to your teens about the situation, start with an appeal to their conscience. Express your deep disappointment in being deceived by someone you love so much—someone in whom you had placed your trust. Explain that seeds of distrust have been sown in all of their relationships. You cannot help but distrust their friends because they supported the dishonesty.

The repercussion is that your teens will not enjoy the freedom or the privacy they had previously enjoyed. All activities will be monitored by you or someone you trust until trustworthiness is reestablished. Understand that it's your teens' responsibility to make a plan to regain your trust, to present a plan that is acceptable to you, and then carry it out faithfully.

WHAT COULD YOU SAY?

You might say, "I know that lying sometimes seems a viable way out of a difficult situation, but it only ends by destroying relationships. If you continue to lie, it will cost you the relationships you value most. When no one can trust you and you can't even trust yourself, your self-respect goes *out the window*. Above all, deceit will affect the enjoyment of your relationship with God, and I don't want that to happen to you.

"Our being able to trust you is the basis of your freedoms within our family. It's up to you to figure out how you are going to become trustworthy and regain those freedoms. Until then you are grounded from all parties. I am here to help you in any way I can, but I can't make you be truthful. You have to do that on your own. When you're ready to discuss a plan that you think will help, let me know, and we'll talk about it.

"As your parent, I will not lie to you. I will not be perfect, but I will always be honest with you because I love you. I can forgive any mistakes that you may make, but I will not tolerate the ongoing lying."

WISDOM FROM GOD'S WORD

What teenager doesn't want to be free! Tell your teens, "Lying will keep you in bondage, but it is the truth that sets you free."

> The LORD detests lying lips, but he delights in men who are truthful. (Prov. 12:22 NIV)

Additional related resources (audio and print) are available from Hope for the Heart (http://www.hopefortheheart.org/):
Ethics & Integrity; Lying

36

Borrowing

Clothes vanish from closets. Robes disappear from racks. Makeup migrates from drawers. Jewelry jumps from one bedroom to another. Magazines walk away by themselves.

You wonder, *Has my house been the target of a thief? Is there a ghost on the loose?* No, your daughter Bonnie has become a "borrower."

While she freely helps herself to any item she chooses, the rest of the family is reduced to threatening her—or pleading with her—to return their property. They lock away whatever they don't want to lose.

Sometimes this kind of borrowing takes place when teens feel deprived. At other times borrowing is a result of laziness, self-centeredness, or thoughtlessness. They borrow something belonging to someone else without permission, but with every intention of returning it after having used it. Regardless, it is a great irritant to the other members of a household.

To your teens, this topic will doubtless seem ridiculous when you address it. In their view they see no problem. There will likely be no effective reasoning with them because they won't see this as an issue—until it affects them. You will find that this will be one of the times when you have to wear the *black hat*. You need to respectfully but firmly enforce the boundaries that you have set on borrowing and move on!

WHAT COULD YOU DO?

Some parents feel that siblings should be encouraged to share with each other since they are members of the same family and thus dependent on each other. This arrangement is good when it is truly voluntary, but all too often one sibling takes advantage of the other's desire to be generous. Thus you could wind up with one's being a disgruntled doormat and the other a frequent freeloader.

Help your teen see that borrowing without permission from the owner is tantamount to stealing. Proverbs 20:17 (MESSAGE) says, "Stolen bread tastes sweet, but soon your mouth is full of gravel."

Establish early on that other people's property is off-limits. If your teenagers have separate bedrooms, they should be taught not to enter a sibling's room without permission or when that person is absent.

When siblings share a bedroom (or one is significantly younger than the other), territorial lines tend to blur. Sarah, a sixteen-year-old who shared a bedroom with her younger sister Susie, frequently came home to find her cosmetics or jewelry used or missing. The mother's admonitions to Susie were ineffective in lessening the lure of the older teenager's possessions.

Sarah grew increasingly frustrated and angry about having to replace items Susie had ruined. Finally the parents bought Sarah a large footlocker for her room in which she stored everything that seemed to interest Susie. Then Sarah padlocked it and kept the key on her key ring.

As teenagers mature, they need to learn respect for the possessions of others by honoring boundaries. Whether a possession cost time to make or money to buy, respect for property implies an appreciation for the value of time and money.

Therefore, an effective deterrent to destructive borrowing is to levy a fine. If your teenagers do not receive an allowance and have no access to money, they could "work off" the debt by doing odd jobs around the house. Your ground rules for borrowing might include the following:

- There is to be no borrowing without express *prior* permission.
- Anything borrowed with permission is to be returned to the owner in excellent condition by the agreed-on time. Romans 13:8 says, "Owe no one anything, except to love each other, for the one who loves another has fulfilled the law."
- Anything returned late incurs a monetary fine (such as five dollars), payable to the owner, or an odd job to be completed in a specified period of time.
- Anything returned damaged is to be replaced by the borrower.
- Anything lost, stolen, or destroyed is to be promptly replaced at the borrower's expense.
- Anything borrowed without permission is considered stolen and is subject to the above with an additional, predetermined penalty (such as ten dollars) payable to the owner.

• There will be no more borrowing if any rule is not followed.

Rules like these are a beginning point, nothing more. Your teenagers need to internalize them so that they become second nature and the problem disappears. If you have to invoke the rules over and over again, then the rules are evidently not working. They may require tweaking in order to be practical for your household. Before you scrap them altogether, however, consider whether they are being enforced consistently and uniformly. Erratic application is usually the reason for a breakdown in the rules.

If your teenagers are borrowing from family members at will, they're probably borrowing from friends too. Pay attention: Are they eating out frequently when you know they don't have the money? (They *may* be mooching off friends.) Is their bedroom floor cluttered with unfamiliar clothes? (They may belong to someone else.)

Investigate by asking questions. Your teens might admit that the clothes are Jill's but insist that Jill doesn't mind because "she's got a ton of stuff." In fact, Jill herself may not notice or mind, but the parent paying for her clothes will likely be asking, "Where is that outfit I bought for you last week?" When Jill replies that your daughter Bonnie has it, you can count on her mother's insisting that Jill ask for it back. If she later receives a wadded-up bundle to wash and iron, she may even be put in the awkward position of contacting you to ask for replacement or reimbursement of the cleaning bill. When it gets to this point, it has gone too far.

In a situation such as this, see to it that the borrowed items are promptly returned in *excellent condition*—by you, if necessary—and that borrowed money is paid back in full. Then work it out with your teen to reimburse you.

WHAT COULD YOU SAY?

"Bonnie, we're committed to providing what you truly need, and it's our joy to provide occasional things that you want. But your habit of borrowing things from others concerns me. If we aren't providing what you need, then talk to us.

"I don't want you to be seen by your friends as a moocher. I want you to be a person who respects the property of others and who is responsible enough to carry your own load and pay your own way. Right now you've developed a reputation of not respecting others or their possessions. When you fail to return borrowed items, you are inviting the distrust of your friends and even of your family.

"From now on, no borrowing unless you talk to me about it first. You will wear clothes from your own closet. And when you are with friends, order only what you have the cash to pay for. If you still choose to borrow, your allowance will be suspended. I know you can change, and I want to do whatever I need to do to help you. You have too much to offer others to let this habit come between you and your friends—and between you and your family."

WISDOM FROM GOD'S WORD

While Scripture encourages giving, borrowing can quickly become a snare and can tie your teenagers to others in a way that damages friendships and other relationships. Explain this passage to them:

The borrower is the slave of the lender. (Prov. 22:7)

Additional related resources (audio and print) are available from Hope for the Heart (http://www.hopefortheheart.org/):
Stealing; Ethics & Integrity

37

Questionable Friends

Your teen has begun to associate with kids whose attitudes and actions concern you. They do poorly in school and wear extreme, antisocial clothing and hairstyles. They are secretive about their activities, and when they do come to your home, it's only to collect your daughter Clare and then take off again. Their parents appear to exert little authority over them, and these kids seem to be encouraging Clare to defy your rules.

WHAT COULD YOU DO?

Talk to your teens about the importance of who they associate with. Proverbs 13:20 says, "Whoever walks with the wise becomes wise, but the companion of fools will suffer harm." Explore together what it means to be a friend (Proverbs 17:17) and how friends treat one another. Philippians 2:4 says, "Let each of you look not only to your own interests, but also to the interests of others."

Plan opportunities to be with your teens' new friends and get to know them personally. See whether it is possible to develop positive relationships with them. Be friendly and nonjudgmental. Find whatever ground you can for connecting with them, whether it's computers, creative efforts, or ideologies. You may be surprised at how well they respond to you.

Often teens who have hostile relationships with their own parents can form good relationships with the parents of their friends. All teens appreciate friends and need mentors who care, even if they're from an older generation and have gray hair! You may never know how profoundly your kindness will affect them for their good. View this as an opportunity for ministry. It could change the course of their lives, not to mention save your daughter from their negative influence.

Ask God to give you a genuine concern for your teens' friends. When the time is right, begin to gently inquire about them. It will be best if you ask specific questions about individuals in the group. Give thought to the questions you want to ask. It might help you to make a list of questions (only for yourself) regarding the friends about whom you are curious. Say the questions out loud before voicing them to your teen. It is important that the questions not sound judgmental. Don't make all your inquiries in one sitting. Make questioning a part of your relationship. If you ask questions in order to understand, they may open up to you about the reasons for their choice of friends.

Avoid preaching. Don't browbeat your teenagers' friends with your faith. Jesus said, "All people will know that you are my disciples, if you have love for one another" (John 13:35)—not if you win arguments about the Bible or demonstrate how morally superior you are. Ask God to reveal their needs that He can meet through you. Look at these young people as potential brothers and sisters in Christ.

If your daughter has a romantic interest in one of these young men, then you will need to use even more tact. Prohibiting her from seeing him could make him all the more attractive to her and provide greater incentive for her to defy you. Instead, let her see you reach out to him. However, it is important that you establish clear boundaries about where and when they can see each other. For example, they can see each other at your home and be with your family, but they cannot go out alone until you get to know and trust him.

If it is your son who is attracted to a girl of questionable character, you have the opportunity to exert far more influence than you realize—if you choose. Mothers, restrain your dislike for this wayward soul and welcome her with open arms. Encourage your son to bring her into your home rather than out on dates, at least until you can trust your son to withstand the temptation to be inappropriate with her. Be warm and courteous. Smile and converse. Say nothing remotely critical. Then one of three things will happen:

- You will win her over with love.
- She will become disgusted with your lifestyle and leave.
- Your son will decide he can do better and break up with her.

Any of these options is better than what you are likely to achieve with frosty disapproval.

I will never forget one woman I met at a conference where I was speaking on forgiveness. During the question-and-answer time, this mother shared about her son. As a young man, he began living an immoral lifestyle with a young woman known for being promiscuous.

As deeply grieved as this mother was by her son's choices and as upset as she could have been at the sight of this "temptress," she could have locked her heart's door and frozen the couple out. But she didn't. Her attitude was that of rare Christlike love. She reached out not just to her son but especially to the young woman. She looked beyond her fault and saw her need for the Lord. Periodically the mother gave her small gifts with Scripture verses attached. She had them over for dinner and kept her door open to them. She lived out the love of Jesus, who said, "Love your enemies" (Matt. 5:44).

Eventually this mother's love won the young woman to the Lord. And in time the son followed suit and became a Christian. They later were married and committed their home to the Lord.

In reference to your daughter's "new friends," use get-togethers with her friends to draw out their positive, likeable attributes—some are there, though you may have to dig deep for them—and build from there.

While you are forming relationships with her friends, you are automatically supervising their activities. If your house becomes "the" place to go, your daughter will be grateful, and you will know where she is and what she is doing.

Just don't be lulled into complacency and regularly leave them unsupervised in a separate part of the house, or you may be unpleasantly surprised to find out why your house has become "the" place to go.

WHAT COULD YOU SAY?

You might say to your teen, "I would like to get to know your friends. Why don't we have them over for pizza and a movie one night? Don't panic, I am not going to embarrass you, but I do want to spend some time getting to know them. I want to know them because they are important to you and because you like them. What do you think they would enjoy?"

It may be that after everything you try, you discover one in the group to be an incorrigible liar, abusive of your trust, or possessing the conscience of a split pea. In that case you are justified in telling your daughter, "I gave Josh every chance I could, but it seems he's mostly interested in trying to play me for a fool. I'm not a fool, and I love you too much to let your life go down the tubes with his. His choices have left me with no other option but to say he's no longer welcome. I will continue to ask God to bring good into his life, but I can't see any good in your continuing a relationship with him." If you have been sincere in your efforts up until now, your daughter will understand. She may even be indignant at Josh's duplicity.

WISDOM FROM GOD'S WORD

Friends are vital to teenagers. Who those friends are is even more vital. Help your teens learn the importance of choosing wisely the company they keep . . . their influencers, their molders and shapers.

> Do not be deceived: "Bad company ruins good morals." (1 Cor. 15:33)

Additional related resources (audio and print) are available from Hope for the Heart (http://www.hopefortheheart.org/):

Friendship

38

Unknown Friend's Party

It's Friday afternoon, and your son calls you at work. "Dad, can I go to a party tonight at Chad's?"

"Chad? Who's Chad? I don't know him," you respond.

"Oh, he's this guy at school. Please? All my friends will be there—Seth and Danny and Jarrod—you know them . . . they're okay. Please? I need to know now so I can get a ride with Seth. I've done all my chores, and you said you were really proud of me for making an A on that physics test. Please, Dad?"

You really want to make the right call here. But who is this Chad?

WHAT COULD YOU DO?

Matthew 10:16 says, "Behold, I am sending you out as sheep in the midst of wolves, so be wise as serpents and innocent as doves."

Here is the experience of one Kansas family as related by the dad:

Our second son was eager to try out his expanded social life in the eighth grade by asking our permission to attend a friend's party one Friday evening. My wife and I asked, "Are the parents there?" and our son automatically responded, "Yes."

After dropping him off at the friend's house, we began to have doubts about the level of supervision at the party. We decided to call the house. A young boy answered, and I asked to speak to the father. I heard him ask away from the phone, "Does anyone have a deep voice?" Another boy got on the phone and made a lame attempt to sound like an adult. I hung up, looked at my wife, and we both said, "We're going over there."

We arrived at the house only to spot our son "making out" with a girl right in front of the living room window. We rang the doorbell, collected our son, and quickly exited with one upset and embarrassed young man in tow. After that incident, he realized that we meant business concerning

219

his social life. He spent the next weekend at home, and for the next six months we confirmed all of his information with other parents.

To avoid having this happen in your family, when your teens wish to attend a party, you might start by having them put a responsible adult on the phone, one who knows the parents of the teen who is having the party. Get what preliminary information you can about the family's values and lifestyle. In addition, many high schools offer some kind of a Parent Pledge. This is an optional contract that states parents will permit no alcohol, smoking, or drugs at teenage parties in their homes. Students whose parents have signed this pledge are highlighted in the student directory. This gives you a quick and easy reference, and it is a positive place to begin your investigation.

The next step is to call the home where the party is taking place and speak with at least one of the teen's parents. Do not take the teenager's word for it that the party will be chaperoned. (Would he *tell* you if it weren't?) Your teens should understand in advance that if you cannot get one host parent on the phone before the party, they can't go. Next time they'll give you more notice. Talking with a parent will give you a clear idea of their sense of responsibility. It may be embarrassing, time-consuming, and inconvenient to ask, but it may spare you a greater embarrassment and inconvenience later.

You could specifically ask:

- "Will you be there for the party?"
- "Will you be there the entire evening as a chaperone?"
- "Will there be any other adult chaperone?"
- "Will there be any alcohol available or allowed?"
- "Will you be taking responsibility for what goes on?"

How well I remember a seventh-grade party at Button's house. (Button was a smooth talker—even for seventh grade—and he knew how to charm the girls.) About an hour after everyone had arrived, Button's mother and father slipped out—all by design of course—and the bar was open with every kind of imaginable drink. (A tinge stronger than "Shirley Temple" drinks, needless to say!) I'm sure his parents thought they were being cool, but in reality they were irresponsible. You can assume parents will be present for a party at their own home, but as the old saying goes, "It ain't necessarily so."

By the way, I never told either of my parents about the party I attended. Of course I never would have told my father, but I might have told my mother . . . if she had truly probed. Then she could have taught me how to handle future uncomfortable situations. Consider asking your teenagers questions when they come in from a party. Ask them to check with you before they go to bed. That way you will find out not only if they made the curfew, but also if they are acting irrationally or have alcohol on their breath.

Some months ago several hundred parents were called in the middle of the night by the police to come pick up their teenagers at a suburban Dallas warehouse. These teens had been busted at a keg party where there were large quantities of alcohol (there was one keg for every three people). All the teens apprehended at the warehouse were charged with underage drinking, and those over twenty-one were charged with providing alcohol to minors.

Parents had to post on-the-spot bail and sign an agreement to appear in court before they could take their children home. And because the suburban school district has a zero-tolerance alcohol and drug policy, the students faced disciplinary action ranging from suspension to expulsion, depending on the severity of the charge and each student's past behavior. One of the police officers interviewed at the scene said in disgust, "Not one of these parents knew where their kid was tonight. Well, now they know."

Make your teenagers a part of establishing the rules. You and your teens should have a clear understanding when it comes to parties. Then enforce the agreed-upon rules, even if it means they can't go. Don't make them feel like victims when that happens. Brainstorm alternative entertainment involving other friends or family members. Ownership affords a sense of responsibility, and your child will eventually take decision making more seriously. Proverbs 9:12 (NIV) says, "If you are wise, your wisdom will reward you."

WHAT COULD YOU SAY?

You might say, "I understand how much you want to go to this party since your friends will be there, and I want you to be able to have a good time too. So I need you to take the initiative in getting one of Sean's or Jarrod's parents on the phone, whichever one knows the family situation of the boy giving the party. After that conversation, if I like what I hear, then I'll need the phone number of the boy's parents. I'll find out what I need to know about the party from them. After that, you and I will talk about what I've learned and make a decision as to whether it's a good idea for you to go or not. If it works out, great. If it doesn't, then maybe we can figure out something else that would be fun to do. If you want to have some friends over here, I'll provide the pizza." Psalm 37:30 says, "The mouth of the righteous man utters wisdom, and his tongue speaks what is just" (NIV).

WISDOM FROM GOD'S WORD

It requires strength of character for teenagers to heed the warning in their spirit and say no to a fun time with the "in" crowd. Sometimes danger can be seen, and sometimes it can only be felt. In either case, share with your teenagers the wisdom of not proceeding when there are danger signals.

> The prudent sees danger and hides himself, but the simple go on and suffer for it. (Prov. 22:3)

Additional related resources (audio and print) are available from Hope for the Heart (http://www.hopefortheheart.org/):

Friendship

39

Refusing Extracurricular Activities

Your son, who has never given you trouble before, starts refusing to participate in any group activity. Although he is good at basketball, he won't consider trying out for a team. He likes to play chess, but only online; he is not willing to play with a person across the table. Scouting is out—he refuses to wear a uniform. In fact, it seems that he has an excuse to avoid joining any organization, and you are concerned that he's missing out on something that could be important to his life.

In general, sports, clubs, and organized volunteer activities are valuable opportunities for social growth, especially for teens. They help build social skills, physical skills, confidence, and camaraderie. Occasionally, however, a teen simply refuses to participate in any organized activity.

WHAT COULD YOU DO?

Pray that you will be sensitive and discerning regarding the reasons for your teen's acting this way. Has he always been somewhat reclusive? The jolt of entering adolescence may make him retreat even further. Has he always been self-conscious? His sudden physical changes may make him cringe at the thought of running onto a field under the scrutiny of hundreds of eyes. Is he afraid to try new things? Is he afraid of rejection? Does he insist everything be done his way? Is he sensitive to criticism?

Your teen may not tell you the real reasons for his reluctance. He may not be fully aware of them himself. You'll need to be very prayerful and perceptive to find these reasons, but it's important that you do. Avoid giving an ultimatum that he participate or else!

Your teen's refusal to participate may be a sign that his schedule is overloaded. You may need to sit down with your teen and evaluate every activity in which he is involved and help him prioritize his time. One parent took her son out of every activity, even youth group, because he was manifesting signs of overload. After his life became more balanced, they began to slowly add in one activity at a time until they found what was right for him. More is not always better, and often less is more, as the expression goes.

One teen's parents decided church and music activities for the family were nonnegotiable. Aside from that, their teens were allowed to select only one additional activity in which to participate. If they managed it well, they could come and present their case for why they wanted to add another. Together the parents and teen would weigh the pros and cons of adding another activity. If grades did not suffer and the teen was getting enough rest and wasn't showing signs of stress, then another activity would be tried. This kept the extracurricular activities from becoming out of control and avoided the teen's experiencing failure and having to cut back again.

If the reasons amount to immaturity or fears that your son can overcome, then you have more work to do. Investigate the group activities offered through his school. Belonging to a group gives him an identity at school, friends with common interests, and a reason to look forward to the school day. Try to persuade him to join a group on a trial basis. Resort to rewards, if necessary. One mother of a shy, withdrawn girl offered to buy her an expensive pair of jazz shoes if she would take dance class in high school. This led to a place on the drill team and later to a leadership position.

Unfortunately, some kids feel so disenfranchised from their school (and some schools are so mercilessly controlled by cliques) that a teen may feel it is impossible to fit in there. The next step is community groups. Encourage your son to run an Internet search on topics that interest him, or send him to your local librarian for help. Whatever field he finds—robotics, philately, trebuchets, or some other nonconventional topics—there's going to be a group somewhere for him to try on for size. Obviously you will not drop him off just anywhere. Go with him until you are satisfied that the group is a healthy outlet for him. Keep abreast of his activities and accomplishments.

There are few things sadder than a child who pursues competence in a stimulating field about which his parents are totally uninformed.

It may be that after all of your research, encouragement, and trial runs, your child's activities fall off again, and he is back to spending most of his time in his room. In this case you need to know exactly how he is occupying himself. If it's reading, find out what kind of books he enjoys and guide him to appropriate material. If it's writing or drawing, ask to see his work. Some kids who have deep, introspective minds and a creative bent simply need time alone to nurture their gift.

Paul told the Philippians, "Let each of you look not only to his own interests, but also to the interests of others" (Phil. 2:4).

If this is what your son is doing, you will recognize it by the quality of material he turns out. Some kids who are truly called of God to a special purpose will feel the need to cloister, to spend a great deal of time alone wrestling with their God-given purpose, seeking understanding and strength from Him. If you see that your child is truly marching to the beat of a different drummer and needs silence to hear the far-off music, you would be wise to find out what teacher could help develop his skills.

WHAT COULD YOU SAY?

Take your teen out for a burger and a milk shake. Talk about what interests him or her. Brainstorm different options. Listen to what your teen has to say. Bear in mind that introverts are wary of being with people. They need to be alone to recharge. If your teen is an introvert, being at school all day may be exhausting, and quiet time at home is needed to recharge. It may not be a lack of interest in extracurricular activities as much as simple exhaustion. In which case, it is better *not* to encourage extra activities. Listen to what your teen is *really* saying and needing.

Ask, "What helps you unwind after a hard day or week at school? Do you prefer to hang out in your room and be quiet? Or hang out with just one or two friends? Read? Listen to music? Or do you like to be with lots of friends? Have you thought about where you might like to be in ten years? Are there things you may want to do now that would help you get to where you want to be in your future?" Gently inquire with a few questions, and then back off and let your teen do the talking. The reflections, thoughts, and dreams shared may give you an insight as to what extracurricular activities should be a part of the schedule.

"I know God created you for a purpose, and I want to do all I can to help you develop His purpose. What do you want to do in life? And what are you doing to develop the talents and interests God has given you? I know that God has made you special and unique, and I wouldn't want to change you for anything in the world. I do feel responsible to help you develop to your full potential. Take some time to think about it. Let's pray about what gives you the greatest sense of joy and fulfillment. Then let's plan a way to develop your potential." Ephesians 2:10 (NIV) tells us, "We are God's workmanship, created in Christ Jesus to do good works, which God prepared in advance for us to do."

WISDOM FROM GOD'S WORD

Make a concerted effort to interest your teenagers in nurturing friendships. Share the importance of your friends and their benefit to you. Recount the story of David and Jonathan. David's son Solomon wrote these words about the importance of friends:

> Two are better than one, because they have a good return for their work: If one falls down, his friend can help him up. But pity the man who falls and has no one to help him up! (Eccles. 4:9–10 NIV)

Additional related resources (audio and print) are available from Hope for the Heart (http://www.hopefortheheart.org/):
Friendship, Purpose in Life

40

Refusing Church Participation

Your otherwise pleasant teenage son suddenly decides that he doesn't want to go to church anymore. Since you insist that Ronnie go, Sunday morning has turned into a battle of wills that ruins the sanctity of the day. "I have friends who don't go to church," he snaps back. "Are you saying that none of them have any moral character? They are better people than everybody in the church!" Ronnie's refusal distresses you, for you know he needs biblical morality and Christian character—he needs Christ now more than ever. But Ronnie is adamant that he does not want to go and will not go.

WHAT COULD YOU DO?

Remember two key characteristics of young adolescents. First, as they begin to find their identity separate from you as parents, they often see only the inconsistencies of the adult world. Second, they are disputatious—they would argue with a stump. As parents, this becomes wearisome in every area, but when it comes to the things of God, it can be especially disconcerting. It's a comfort to know that deep down your teen has a place that only God can fill.

God is about relationships, and He desires a personal relationship with your teens. Teens want to be *connected*. The more you can keep the church issue on a relational level, the better chance you have of reaching them. For example, you may consider driving some of their friends to church. Take them to eat after church or youth group. Teens rarely turn down an opportunity to be with their friends and get a free meal.

Listen to your teens. There may be a good reason they do not want to go. Is the youth group boring? Is the teaching irrelevant or unbiblical? Is there a problem with gossip or bullying? Is the youth group "alive" or "dead"? Is there true Bible study?

Ask about the real reason they don't want to go to church.

More alarming, is someone at church making your teens uncomfortable? Much as we would like to believe that the church—any church—is a safe place for our children, Scripture warns us that emissaries of Satan can worm their way into otherwise good churches. (See Rev. 2:14, 20.) And newspaper headlines about church leaders who are forced to resign under the weight of evidence of impropriety are distressingly frequent. To go yourself is the only way for you to really know what any particular church group is like. It may be that a change of churches is in order.

You may find it helpful to come right out and ask, "Has anything ever happened at church or with anyone from the church where you found yourself sexually pressured or morally compromised? Do you know of any sexual abuse? Are you uncomfortable being around anyone there?" Obviously if the answer is yes, get the details and report it immediately. Those issues having been directly addressed, the real reason for the rebellion, most likely, is an issue of the heart.

If you are satisfied that the problem does not lie with the church, then it's time to tactfully talk to your teens. Don't be dictatorial, self-righteous, or legalistic about attendance at every church function, but help them prioritize which activities are the most important.

Some teens, in line with the postmodern culture that saturates their world, may choose a worship style that is different from the one in your church. While you may prefer a more traditional worship service and music, they may prefer a more interactive or contemporary style of worship and music. This choice does not negate their love for the Lord—the worship style is just different.

Sometimes as parents of postmodern teens, we lose them in our desire to get them to conform to our world. Perhaps the best way to *bond* is to give them an extended *boundary* as long as it is within the parameters of what you believe. For example, you may not allow a New Age church but will allow one, though different from yours, that is Christian and biblically based.

You may want to consider encouraging your teens to be involved in another ministry. Many teenagers have been reached through parachurch organizations—Christian camps, Young Life, Youth for Christ, choir and missions tours, youth Bible studies, Christian volunteer organizations. Pray that your teenagers would develop strong friendships with authentic believers—wise Christian friends who will sharpen them and make them wise. Proverbs 13:20 says, "Whoever walks with the wise becomes wise."

At one point my father forbade Mother and the four of us children to go to church. I was sixteen at the time. The year before, we had joined a vibrant, biblically based church, and I genuinely believe my father was feeling that the church was in competition with him.

Although my mother was typically a tenderhearted, submissive woman, on this one point she did not yield. She negotiated that she would stay home with him, but we children had to be in church. She believed with all her heart that she would be failing as a parent if she didn't make her top priority the training we would receive from wonderful Bible teachers.

The words she used with me were, "When you are raising children, church is a nonnegotiable. Children will be taught values that will last a lifetime. And of greatest importance," she said, "they must come to know the Lord." Nothing was more important than experiencing a life-changing relationship with Jesus. I thank God for a mother who numerous times, sometimes to her own hurt, prioritized what was truly best for us.

WHAT COULD YOU SAY?

Years ago when I was a youth director, I gave many parents a logical, practical approach on how to talk to their teens with tact. Before you meet with your teenagers, pray for God to prepare their hearts and to speak through you. "A wise man's heart guides his mouth, and his lips promote instruction" (Prov. 16:23 NIV).

Practice this approach:

- More and more, I'll be giving you greater freedom to make your own choices, and one day you'll be out on your own, making all of your own decisions.
- But for now, God has given me the privilege of having you under my protection and direction.
- Do you want me to try to do what is pleasing to God? Wait for a response. It should be affirmative.
- My highest priority is to please God, especially where it concerns you.
- Because I deeply love you, I want to please you, too. However, I know there will be times I can't do both.

- In this case, it would be wrong for me to say you don't need to go to church. The truths that are taught there are going to be crucial for you to know, especially when you're out on your own. You know, God will hold me accountable for how I raise you.
- In our family, we go to church. Church is where we, as believers, join with others to worship, celebrate Communion, hear God's Word taught, pray, serve, fellowship, and grow. Going to church isn't my idea—it's God's.
- First Corinthians 12:7 (NLT) says, "A spiritual gift is given to each of us so we can help each other." And Galatians 6:10 says, "So then, as we have opportunity, let us do good to everyone, and especially to those who are of the household of faith." Going to church enables us to get to know those in the household of faith, so we can use our spiritual gifts and other resources to help them. And it enables them to do the same for us when we have a need. In this way, everyone benefits. It's God's plan.
- Let's look for at least one thing we can learn and then talk about together. Encourage open and honest dialogue. It is healthy for your teens to have questions about God. If you have discussions with them, it helps them to stay invested and interested. If you tell them not to question the things of God, you are pushing them toward the exit door. The goal is for your teens to have an *authentic* relationship with the living God through knowing Jesus Christ, His Son. When you model an open, honest, transparent relationship with your teens, you model the path for their authentic relationship with the Lord.
- Let's both go to the services, learn as much as we can, and pray that we'll come away with at least one truth we can put to good use during the week. Okay?

WISDOM FROM GOD'S WORD

Sometimes the purpose of going to church is obscured by the routine practice of going to church. If your teenagers are balking at continuing "the practice," do your part to make sure your church is meeting the purpose that the author of the book of Hebrews outlined:

> Let us consider how to stir up one another to love and good works, not neglecting to meet together, as is the habit of some, but encouraging one another, and all the more as you see the Day drawing near. (Heb. 10:24–25)

Additional related resources (audio and print) are available from Hope for the Heart (http://www.hopefortheheart.org/):

The Bible: Is It Reliable?; God; Who Is He?; The Holy Spirit; Jesus; Is He God?; Atheism & Agnosticism

41

Violence

You're at work. It's late morning. Your phone rings. "Did you hear about the shooting? It's at the high school. I heard someone's dead!"

Shooting? Dead? Who's dead . . . and who did it? You can't breathe. . . .

You run outside, jump into the car, and speed toward the school just twelve blocks away. Frantic for news, you scan the dial . . . the first, scant details are starting to air.

A gang of students started a fight on school property, tempers flared, and now a student is dead.

After arriving at school, you learn that the boy was in your son's class—both high school seniors. Your eyes scan the crowd. *Where is my son? . . . Where is my boy?*

The principal is now staring at you . . . and starts walking your way. You are scared spitless! *Is your son the shooter?* You cry out to God, *Please let my son be okay. . . . Don't let my boy be in that gang . . . I beg you, God, before it's too late. . . . please.*

This scenario cuts right to the heart of every parent who has a child in school. Safety is always at the top of the list of parental concerns.

Violence is escalating everywhere, and it has been a trap for teenagers. Senseless violence streams in from their virtual video worlds where they can "seek, kill, and destroy" anyone at will, where terrorist attacks and beheadings are viewed like the nightly news, where video games display women as sex objects to be raped. They see it, hear it, feel it . . . and eventually want to do it!

And now research is showing an alarming *desensitization* to violence in the brain. Specifically, the brains of teens who are exposed to excessive electronic violence are revealing an unfeeling crop of youth that lack compassion, care, and empathy for others. One clear fruit of these teens is that they simply *do not care!*[1]

And if the media frenzy of violence becomes fueled by other factors—depression and drugs, dysfunction and divorce—then gangs are even more alluring to teens.

Common contributors to violent gang membership include:

• abusive families
• access to guns
• addiction issues
• alcohol and drug abuse
• broken homes
• excessive media violence
• unresolved anger
• untreated depression

Common characteristics of violent gang members are:

• aggression
• commitment
• connection
• fear
• honor
• pride
• tradition
• turf/territory

WHAT COULD YOU DO?

The best plan to prevent your teens from participating in acts of violence is to know their hearts. Violent acts don't happen randomly. Almost always an escalating series of emotions and events precipitate violent behavior.

Be Pro-active at Home

• Spend quality time together as a family. Stay connected to your teens by taking them out to eat on a regular basis . . . even if just for pizza, an ice cream cone, or a hamburger.
• Invite your teens' friends to your home, and make it a fun place to be. Be friendly, but don't try to "be their friend." Stay home; don't leave to give them space. Be the best parent you can possibly be.
• Know where your teens are going and with whom.
• Set curfews with a boundary that should not be crossed. If the time of the curfew is exceeded, enact repercussions.

- Pay attention to possible negative changes you see in your teens, and respond appropriately. And if necessary, get them professional help.
- As a parent, you need to be involved in the life of your teens and know about the security of their world.

Be Proactive at School

- Place a high value on education—verbally.
- Get involved in the parent-teacher organization.
- Volunteer to help when the school asks.
- Know the school's plans for prevention of violence and procedures for lockdowns.

After a Violent Act—Not Gang-related

If your teen has committed a violent act but doesn't appear to be involved with a gang, put the following measures into place:

- Establish *repercussions* that are related to the violent behavior. Teenagers must replace any damaged property with money they themselves have earned. And they must make *restitution* in person. Likewise, they must *restore* damaged relationships, if at all possible. Specifically, if someone has been hurt, your teen must seek forgiveness.
- There must be an all-out effort to do specific acts of service and other constructive acts to show goodwill.

Gang Involvement

- If you suspect that your teen is becoming involved with a gang, you must intervene immediately. Once he is deeply entrenched or if indoctrination develops into contempt for authority figures, his fear may prevent any attempt on his part to detach from the gang. If you are afraid of your teen, you may have to bring in professionals, including the police. Typically, gang members will stop at nothing to prevent another member from leaving. Proceed with utmost caution.
- Your primary concern is to get your teen free of the gang's deadly grip. You may have to take precautionary measures to protect the safety of your teen during this time. Psalm 82:4 says, "Rescue the weak and the needy; deliver them from the hand of the wicked." Counseling will be needed as part of the healing process.

WHAT COULD YOU SAY?

The old adage is true: "Love" is often spelled t-i-m-e. In a neutral setting and not in an interrogation style, talk with your teens about gangs. "Would you help me understand why kids get into gangs? [Allow time for an answer.] What can I do to help you so that you won't be drawn into gang life? Do any of your friends need us to reach out to them? What suggestions do you have for me?"

Most important is your interest and involvement in the life of your teens on a practical level as well as a personal level. Dialogue with your teens. "What do people do at your school during a lockdown?" Ask your teens what they know about security procedures at places such as the mall or theater. "What would you do if something happened?"

If you talk with the attitude that says you are seeking information and brainstorming (as you are), your teens are more likely to be open with you.

Staying connected to teenagers is not always easy since they are often functioning from the emotion center of the brain—and these emotions can be volatile. Often teens are sullen, silent, and moody, making communication feel like a *one-way street.* As a parent, avoid reacting to their negative attitudes by retreating or with the rationalization that they don't want to talk.

Answers to questions such as, "Would you know what to do if someone approached you about being in a gang?" are essential if you are concerned about your teens. But you can't ask them in the same way you invite, "Tell me about your day at school." Teens won't share their hearts until you have been willing to share your time. To gain their trust, they need to know you truly care. Giving of your time is one of the best ways to express your heartfelt commitment to them.

Above all, continually impart the Word of God into the life of your teens. Look for every opportunity to teach them to always put the well-being of another person first. Life is precious and needs to be guarded by God's truths. Jesus said, "I tell you the truth, whoever hears my *word* and believes him who sent me has eternal *life* and will not be condemned; he has crossed over from death to *life*. . . . The *words* I have spoken to you are spirit and they are *life*" (John 5:24; 6:63 NIV, italics added).

WISDOM FROM GOD'S WORD

This is what the LORD says: Do what is just and right. Rescue from the hand of his oppressor the one who has been robbed. Do no wrong or

> violence to the alien, the fatherless or the widow, and do not shed innocent blood in this place. (Jer. 22:3 NIV)

Additional related resources (audio and print) are available from Hope for the Heart (http://www.hopefortheheart.org/):

Anger; Violence; Prejudice; How to Handle Your Emotions

42

Sexual Activity

You shuffle into the kitchen with an armful of groceries. As you slide the bags onto the counter, you hear a crashing thud, followed by trickles of trinkets spilling from your seventeen-year-old's purse. Scooping up the contents, you make sure her cell phone isn't broken. Relieved, you keep gathering the items . . . that is, until you spy a round plastic case.

Immediately you recognize the packaging—birth control pills! Now you realize something is indeed broken—your heart—hurt with the knowledge that your precious daughter is possibly, probably, sexually active.

You've just received tangible proof that your child is engaging in or contemplating sexual intercourse. If condoms had just spilled from your ninth-grader's backpack, you couldn't have been more surprised . . . or hurt.

Our culture sends many sexual messages: Sex is good, being sexy is better, being wanted for sex is best. Our society says, "No problem exists as long as the sexual 'rules of engagement' are understood by both parties." The modern morality in culture says, "Have safe sex." Oh, really?

Safe sex is a myth, and the myth of "safe" sex is not only dangerous but also life-threatening. Assuming that condoms can guarantee safe sex is woefully naive. Realize, every two to four condoms out of a hundred slip down, slip off, leak, or break.[1] Ask yourself, "Would I use a parachute that I knew would fail two out of every one hundred times?" (That's a no-brainer!)

Sexual activity is "safe" only when a sexually pure couple join together in marriage and remain faithful to each other. True love protects 100 percent of the time. Ultimately abstinence is an act of true love that protects every part of a person—body, soul, and spirit. Proverbs 2:11 says, "Discretion will watch over you, and understanding will guard you."

Sadly, school-sponsored sexual education doesn't mean teens are making better choices. Every teenager needs to face this fact: No contraceptive is 100 percent effective, and no "protection" can guarantee safety from sexually transmitted diseases (STDs). Even if a condom is used, the possibility of lifelong emotional and physical damage exists. Abstinence is the only safe alternative.

Sexual images come at us from every direction. Teens are even using cell phones to send sexually explicit messages, photos, and videos. This is child pornography, a serious felony that can result in criminal prosecution and imprisonment. Regrettably these are freeze-framed in the minds of teens, and they are addicting. Sexual addiction, once thought to be a predominantly male issue, has grown to epidemic proportions, affecting old and young, male and female alike.

The sex drives of teens are primarily physical, susceptible to impulsive actions powered by the rush of hormones that flood their bodies at puberty. The rush of testosterone in boys presses them toward physical response. Girls yearn for affection, warmth, and affirmation that they are desirable. Each looks to the opposite sex to meet these needs. But seeking to meet those needs outside of God's ideal corrupts body, mind, and spirit.

Many in our culture no longer consider sex sacred but rather recreational. Some teens push the envelope of propriety by promiscuity. They experiment with homosexual behavior, "hook up" (where "friends with benefits" engage in sex merely for the sake of sex), and attend "rainbow parties" (where group participants using different colored lipstick engage in oral sex). Both girls and boys are encouraged by the culture to be sexually aggressive.

Teens of both genders do have legitimate needs for love, significance, and security.[2] These needs are first met within family relationships and then ultimately in a relationship with God through the Lord Jesus Christ.

WHAT COULD YOU DO?

In a highly sexualized culture, teens are well aware of sex. They are getting an education about sex, but without moral values attached. As a parent, your goal is not merely to instruct your teen to abstain from sex but to treasure purity . . . to honor God in body, mind, and spirit. How do you do that?

• Establish a home where God is loved and honored in word and deed.

Demonstrate and verbalize a healthy marriage between a loving husband and wife. Love and value each child as a blessed gift from God. Discuss God's plan with your children from the time they are small. Hebrews 13:4 says, "Let marriage be held in honor among all, and let the marriage bed be undefiled, for God will judge the sexually immoral and adulterous."

• Establish sexual standards.

Continue discussing with your teens why God's way is best. Spend time teaching them God's perspective on sex. Research shows numerous "teachable moments" are more effective than a one-time sex talk.[3] Ongoing straight talk can encourage your teens to choose abstinence until marriage. Teens must be encouraged and given permission to say no.

If you are a single parent, lead by example and abide by the same standards of sexual purity you expect from your teens. A biblical worldview will help them get through the maze of our sex-saturated society.

First Corinthians 6:18 (NIV) says, "Flee from sexual immorality. All other sins a man commits are outside his body, but he who sins sexually sins against his own body."

Share how God's plan of sexual purity will protect your teens:

• *Emotionally*: They will experience freedom from guilt, anxiety, grief, emotional scars.
• *Physically*: They will be protected from premarital pregnancy, an unwanted child, sexual disease, abortion.
• *Socially*: They will enjoy positive relationships, positive self-image, positive values, positive reputation.
• *Spiritually*: They will live with a pure conscience before God, a pure vision for God's will, a pure motive initiated by God, a pure relationship with God.

Psalm 37:5–6 (NIV) says, "Commit your way to the LORD; trust in him and he will do this: He will make your righteousness shine like the dawn, the justice of your cause like the noonday sun."

• Set practical sexual boundaries.

Monitor and limit the sexual content of music, movies, television, and other entertainment. Install filtering software on your computer, but realize that you can't control every computer available to your child. Encourage group outings as opposed to one-on-one dating, which invites accelerated intimacy. Don't allow opposite-sex teens to be alone in your home or in a room while you are in another. Share the facts about teen sexuality, including statistics regarding venereal diseases, rape, pregnancy, and other consequences.

Encourage your teens by explaining that the Bible has established boundaries regarding sexual activity. Ask them to commit to reading a chapter a day from the book of Proverbs and to write out all the verses that refer to sex.

Proverbs 6:27 (NIV) says, "Can a man scoop fire into his lap without his clothes being burned?"

• If boundaries have been broken . . .

If you know or suspect that your teens are promiscuous, ask about the possibility of childhood sexual abuse. Do not turn away from the answers, no matter how unpleasant. The Lord brings healing, but only when the truth is brought to light. The truth sets us free!

Many teens believe that if you don't have intercourse, you are still a virgin. The word *virgin* means "chaste, unsullied, free from impurity or stain."[4] Teens use the term *born-again virgin* to refer to those who have lost their virginity, either forcibly through molestation or through consensual sex, but later commit to sexual purity. However, "true purity is not some point on a sexual scale. It's a direction, a persistent, determined pursuit of righteousness."[5]

If you suspect your teens have been sexually active but aren't positive, don't accuse them of sexual activity without proof or absolute certainty, or their trust in you could be shattered.

If you *know* your teens have been sexually active, schedule a trip to the doctor immediately for them to be tested for disease.

> This is the will of God, your sanctification: that you abstain from sexual immorality; that each one of you know how to control his own body in holiness and honor. (1 Thess. 4:3–4)

WHAT COULD YOU SAY?

Share the responsibilities that go along with being sexually active, such as raising a child born outside of marriage. Don't focus only on the negatives of premarital sex: affirm the joy of a satisfying sex life in a committed, permanent relationship. Point out, "No one wants to be a divorce statistic; yet those who have had premarital sex are far more likely to get divorced than those who wait until marriage to consummate the relationship."

Tell your teens, "God made your body, and in His eyes it is good. Now I know that I can't control what you do with it, but until you are an adult, I am involved in your choices. As you reach adulthood, *you* become responsible for your own choices. I want you to recognize your God-given worth."

Tell your teens, "God has made it clear through His Word and I have learned by observation that sex outside of marriage has major pitfalls. It robs you of the joy of experiencing sexual fulfillment with your spouse alone. I realize that your own life experience may not have convinced you of that yet, so you're left to decide whether you or God knows best. In the right context, sex is good—it's wonderful. It's a beautiful gift for expressing love, intimacy, and commitment. And it's the means by which life is conceived, a gift from God."

If your teen has been sexually active, pray and ask for God's wisdom and words—that His love and yours would come across clearly when you discuss this with your teen. Ideally, both parents should be present, if possible. If not, it might be less awkward if the mom talks to the daughter or the father with the son.

Regardless of your situation, confirm your love and emphasize that *nothing* your teen does could diminish this love. You want God's best for your teen. You are concerned. Gently begin by saying, "Yesterday I accidentally found (pills, condoms, etc.)."

Wait for a response. If none is given, tenderly say, "You are precious in God's eyes and in mine, too. It is my heart's desire that you follow the Lord's leading in *all* aspects of your life, and having sexual integrity is an important part of God's plan for you. By design, the Lord created our bodies for pleasure and procreation—but only within the sacred relationship of marriage.

"God's instructions are clear. If you are having sex, I believe your choice is wrong, no matter how right it may feel. You are subjecting yourself to serious repercussions, some of which are harmful and can threaten your health *and* your life. As your parent, it is my job to protect you, even from your own decisions."

Their reaction will determine your response. Your aim is to gain insight into the actions and to impart wisdom.

Give your teen a chance to talk.

If your teen offers no response, ask the following:

- Do you want God's blessing on your life? (Read Rom. 12:1–2.)
- Do you want true peace in your heart? (Read Phil. 4:8–9.)
- Do you want to live a life of integrity (being the same in the dark as in the light)? (Read 1 Chron. 29:17.)
- Do you realize that God has given you His power to live a godly life? (Read 2 Pet. 1:3.)
- Do you want to take the place of God in another's person's life? (Read Deut. 5:7; Matt. 22:37.)
- Do you want to protect your relationship with God? (Read Ps. 66:18.)
- Do you want others to follow your example morally? (Read 1 Tim. 4:12.)

WISDOM FROM GOD'S WORD

A sexually active teenager with untamed desires can be like an untamed bronco in a corral—full of energy but nowhere to go. When taking a bronco out of a corral, you use a bridle and blinders to direct the bronco's attention to the open gate and then guide him to pursue freedom beyond the gate. As you talk your teenager out of the corral of illicit sex, direct his or her attention to God's Word in order to go God's way. Guide your teenager to pursue freedom through a relationship with Christ.

> Flee youthful passions and pursue righteousness, faith, love, and peace, along with those who call on the Lord from a pure heart. (2 Tim. 2:22)

Additional related resources (audio and print) are available from Hope for the Heart (http://www.hopefortheheart.org/):

Sexual Addiction; Sexual Integrity; Childhood Sexual Abuse; Rape Recovery; Homosexuality; Guilt; Intimacy; Dating; Temptation; Unplanned Pregnancy

FIGURE 42–1

An STD is an infection that is transmitted through sexual activity, whether vaginal, anal, or oral sex or intimate skin-to-skin contact, from one person who is infected to another person.

- **Bacterial STD**s can be cured with antibiotics.
- **Viral STD**s can never be cured. Symptoms, such as sores or warts, can be treated, but the virus remains in the body, causing the symptoms to flare up again and again.

In the sixteenth century, syphilis was the only identified venereal disease. Then, in the nineteenth century, gonorrhea joined syphilis as a cause of infertility. Both were classified as incurable until the discovery of penicillin in 1943, which eradicated VDs as a major public health issue. However, the wild, sexual revolution of the 1960s became a breeding ground for a myriad of STDs (the new label), including chlamydia and HPV in 1976 and HIV/AIDS in the early 1980s. Today there are more than twenty-five STDs.[6] Some common STDs include the following:

CURABLE SEXUALLY TRANSMITTED DISEASES

Disease	Classification	Transmission	Symptoms	Harmful Effects
Chlamydia (the most common bacterial STD	**Bacteria** that is pus-producing	Vaginal, anal, and oral sex Mother to child	**Men and women:** Asymptomatic or: **Men:** Discharge from penis **Women:** May experience discharge and pain when urinating	**Women:** Sterility, Pelvic Inflammatory Disease (PID), risk of contracting HIV/AIDS increased
Gonorrhea (second-most common bacterial STD)	**Bacteria** that is highly infectious	Vaginal, anal, and oral sex Mother to child	**Men and women:** Asymptomatic or: **Men:** Pus from urethra, burning during urination **Women:** Painless sore, rash, fever, fatigue, pus-like discharge	**Men:** Sterility, scarring of urethra and urinary tract problems **Women:** Sterility, Pelvic Inflammatory Disease (PID), damage to heart and brain
Syphilis (oldest known STD)	**Bacteria** that produces highly infectious sores or patches on the genitals or mouth	Vaginal, anal, and oral sex Mother to child	**Men:** Swollen, non-painful ulcers on genitalia, fever, enlarged lymph nodes **Women:** Discharge, burning during urination, venereal-type warts	**Men:** Damage to heart and brain, blindness **Women:** Damage to heart, brain, and nervous system; can cause birth defects or death in newborns **Men and Women:** Death, risk of contracting HIV/AIDS increased

Social Boundaries

Disease	Classification	Transmission	Symptoms	Harmful Effects
Trichomoniasis	**Parasite** that causes genital infection	Vaginal and anal sex Mother to child	**Men and women:** Asymptomatic or: **Men:** Discharge from the penis and burning during urination **Women:** Foul smelling vaginal discharge and genital pain, vaginal bleeding, swelling, and irritation of the genitals, painful urination	**Men and women:** Risk of contracting HIV/AIDS increased **Women:** Premature rupture of membranes that protect a baby in pregnancy and preterm delivery

INCURABLE SEXUALLY TRANSMITTED DISEASES

Disease	Classification	Transmission	Symptoms	Harmful Effects
Genital Herpes (herpes simplex virus) HSV-1 is associated with the mouth. HSV-2 is associated with the genitals.	**Virus** that infects the skin and mucous membrane	Vaginal, anal, and oral sex Congenital	**Men and women:** Asymptomatic or painful blisters or sores on the genitals, buttocks, thighs, or mouth	**Men and women:** Genital ulcers, higher risk of HIV
Hepatitis B	**Virus** that is a common blood-borne infection	Vaginal, anal, and oral sex Needles Congenital	**Men and women:** Asymptomatic or yellow skin/eyes, fatigue, nausea	**Men and women:** Liver damage, cancer, ultimately death
HPV (Human papilloma virus or "genital warts")	**Virus** that infects the skin and mucous membrane	Intimate skin-to-skin Vaginal, anal, and oral sex	**Men:** Wart-like genital growths **Women:** Asymptomatic (may be detected by a pap smear)	**Men:** Cancer of the penis and anus **Women:** Causes 99% of cervical cancer! Genital warts
HIV/AIDS (Human immuno-deficiency virus) (Acquired Immune Deficiency Syndrome)	**Virus** that invades the immune system and destroys it over time	Vaginal, anal, and oral sex Needles	**Men and women:** Asymptomatic or flu-like symptoms (fatigue, fever, aches) initially *Later:* Skin and oral lesions, diarrhea, difficulty breathing (pulmonary infections), difficulty thinking (meningitis)	**Men and women:** Intestinal infections and Candida mouth infections, immune system failure, TB, cancer, and death

Epilogue:
Thinking outside the Box

Innovative, creative, imaginative. These descriptive words seem to be part of the package necessary for great parenting. There is a very real problem with the self-proclaimed experts who say this is "*the* way" to deal with teenage difficulties. They present their one-two-three approach of discipline because that is what helped in their own homes.

Let's face it. Every teenager is different, every parent is different, and every home is different. That's why it is vital for you as a parent to learn to "think outside the box."

Last week on a flight to North Carolina, I was seated next to a delightful woman in her seventies. As we struck up a conversation, I quickly discovered her to be a warm and winsome lady who had overcome many obstacles in life. She told me her husband left her when their children were young, and she was faced with raising several children alone.

"What helped you the most?" I asked.

"Oh, my faith," she replied. "I couldn't have done it without the help of the Lord." She went on to say that her most difficult time came when one particular son became disrespectful in his teenage years and soon began hanging out with the wrong crowd. When he was about sixteen, he decided he was tired of his mother's constraints. He moved out to get an apartment with his band of undesirables.

One day she got a call from a police officer. He told her that one of the boys her son was living with had been arrested for stealing. The police also confiscated a quantity of stolen goods found in the apartment. "Ma'am," the officer said, "we know your son wasn't involved in the thefts. But since he's hanging out with this kid who is such a bad influence, would you like us to keep him in jail overnight just to teach him a lesson?"

"Will he be in a cell with dangerous inmates?" she asked.

"Oh, no," he replied. "But he will be within earshot of some pretty rough language."

"All right then," she said optimistically. "I'll pick him up tomorrow." That night she prayed and prayed that the Lord would use this experience for her son's good.

The following morning she did several errands and basically took her time picking up her son. Intentionally she didn't arrive at the jail until after lunch.

"When they let him out of the cell, he just ran up and hugged me. 'Oh, Mama, I'm so sorry,' he said. 'I want to . . . Mama, I really want to come home. Will you let me come home?' I replied, 'Yes, of course, you can come home,' and I want you to know, we had no more problems after that."

I smiled and thought to myself, *Here is a woman who has lived out the heart of James 5:20 (NIV): "Whoever turns a sinner from the error of his way will save him from death and cover over a multitude of sins."*

This wise mother's approach is an illustration of what I call "thinking outside the box." A very perceptive single mother allowed her son to experience just enough of a repercussion for breaking a boundary. In doing so, she gave him a glimpse of his destiny . . . a dismal destiny if he continued walking down the destructive path he had lightly chosen. The repercussion of "tank time" gave him some greatly needed "think time."

Recently I asked a friend to do a search for the phrase "thinking outside the box" on the Internet. She discovered it was associated with words like innovative, creative, imaginative, original, ingenious, and inspired. Since I had not thought about how I would define the phrase until I arrived at this last chapter, I find these words helpful for communicating what I hope you take to heart from this book. Remember, boundaries are not only external limits with negative consequences for your teens. The goal of boundaries is to build inner character, and inner character produces trustworthiness. And what is trust but the major bonding ingredient of a relationship?

I encourage you to become innovative as you begin to think outside the box when your teens need a little internal motivation to do what is right! Be inventive and imagine ways that will lead your teenagers to not only view but also welcome discipline as the loving hand of God. As a skilled surgeon uses a scalpel to cut away that which brings physical death and to repair injuries to the body, so the Lord uses discipline to remove sinful attitudes that bring inner death—death to relationships—and to heal injuries to the soul and spirit.

That recent encounter with the mother on the plane brought to mind an incident I had completely forgotten. My own sweet mother was a number-one ace in handling difficult situations when we were teenagers. She *definitely* acted outside the box.

As a freshman in high school, I was not yet allowed to date and had very little experience with boys. One evening I answered the phone and heard this deep baritone voice telling me he was a senior at a local school. I asked how he got my number, and he said he was just dialing random phone numbers. His voice was so intriguing we talked for a while. He called back several times, and then he wanted me to meet him after school one day the next week. He was a good deal older than I, and giving no thought to how dangerous this could turn out to be, I agreed to meet him the next Tuesday.

Though I was flattered with the attention, I didn't share my secret with anyone until the night before. From a well of inner excitement, I told my grandmother about the covert rendezvous planned for the next day. And as the school day was drawing to a close that Tuesday afternoon, I was summoned from my classroom early and told my mother was there to take me to a 3:00 PM dentist appointment. I was totally stunned. Mother had not mentioned anything about a dentist appointment on that Tuesday. As we drove away from the school parking lot, not a word was said about the secret rendezvous I was missing, nor was there any hint of disapproval of me in her spirit. We never talked about the incident, but I knew then that Mother was drawing a boundary. She did it in a very ingenious way, without even mentioning my grandmother or letting on that she knew anything of my intentions. If she had informed me that I most certainly could not meet my mystery date or belittled me for being so naive, I would have resented it, felt shamed, and been upset with Granny to boot. To the contrary, as we drove off in the car, I knew my mother loved me! Her intervening boundary did not anger or alienate me. It quieted my soul.

Ready or not, eventually the day comes for every parent to let go. No matter how adequate or inadequate you feel about the way you've done your job of parenting, one day you will wake up to find yourself retired

... or fired! Many parents identify this milestone as the day their teenagers leave home—to go to college, to start a full-time job, or to get married.

Whether or not you can pinpoint that particular day when your "kite took flight," be at peace—even when it seems your child's life is not sailing on the course you would have chosen. You may not have a hand on the string, but Someone does, and He can do a better job at steering than you can. Never give up on or question the innovative, out-of-the-box things God will be doing to shape, mold, and propel your kite into being a "high flyer."

This is a good time to pray.

God, I've done all I can, but I know You are still at work in my teenager's life. Since Your love is greater, stronger, and more enduring than mine, I am trusting You to complete what You began when You gave me this image-bearer. I'm willing to put the future of my child into Your hands because I know Your Word reads, " 'I know the plans I have for you,' declares the LORD, *'plans to prosper you and not to harm you, plans to give you hope and a future' "* (Jer. 29:11 NIV).

I have saved the following little story to share with you in closing this book because it is the most original example of thinking outside the box I have ever heard, and it's too hard to resist laughing at it one more time. The story was in the September 6, 1998, *Dallas Morning News*. Alan Cost could have just suspended his son's driving privileges after the boy received his third speeding ticket and stayed out way too late. Instead he suspended his son's pickup truck—in a tree. Mr. Cost used a backhoe to hoist the back end of sixteen-year-old Stephen's 1986 Chevrolet pickup several feet in the air and used a chain to suspend it from a tree in front of their house along one of the Birmingham suburb's busiest roads. That was on August 29, and Mr. Cost said it would stay there, where all of Stephen's friends could see it, for another week or so. There was a sign in the vehicle's window: "This is what happens when a teenager does not mind." And in smaller letters it said, "May be for sale." Mr. Cost said, "I hate being that rough on the boy, but if he ain't going to listen to me, I have no other choice."

I can hear all of you who are parents of teenagers applauding.

> Do not despise the LORD's discipline and do not resent his rebuke, because the LORD disciplines those he loves, as a father the son he delights in. (Prov. 3:11–12 NIV)

Notes

Chapter 2: The Black Hat

1. John 14:27.
2. Matthew 5:9.
3. Romans 12:18 NIV.
4. Matthew 10:34 NIV.
5. John 8:32.

Chapter 3: Understanding Your Teen

1. *Merriam-Webster Online Dictionary,* s.v. "adolescent"; http://www.m-w.com.
2. David Walsh, *Why Do They Act That Way?* (New York: Free Press, 2004), 65.

Chapter 11: Cell Phone Abuse

1. Kim Kurth, "The GR8 DB8," *Frisco Style Magazine*, Vol. 14, No. 4, September 2009, 31.
2. See an example from The National Coalition for the Protection of Children and Families' *Sex and Cell Phones* booklet, available online at http://www.national-coalition.org/shopcategory.asp?catID=14.

Chapter 13: Media Mania

1. David Walsh, *Why Do They Act That Way?* (New York: Free Press, 2004), 165.

Chapter 14: Internet Hazards

1. For this agreement see, iCare Coalition, "Safe Use Agreement," http://www.icarecoalition.org/safeuseagreement.asp.

Chapter 21: Bullying

1. Barbara Coloroso, *The Bully, the Bullied, and the Bystander* (New York: HarperResource, 2003), 13.
2. See ibid., 13–14.

Chapter 23: Sexual Harassment

1. Texas Council on Family Violence, "75 Percent of Young Texans Affected by Dating Violence" (2006); http://www.tcfv.org/tcfv-content/75-percent-of-young-texans-affected-by-dating-violence/.
2. Ron Snipe, et al., "Recidivism in Young Adulthood, Adolescent Sexual Offenders Grown Up," *Criminal Justice & Behavior*, Vol. 25 (International Association

tion for Correctional and Forensic Psychology, 1998), 109, 117, cited in National Teen Dating Violence Prevention Initiative, "Teen Dating Violence Facts" (American Bar Association, 2006), 1; http://www.abanet.org/unmet/teendating/facts.pdf.

Chapter 26: Stealing

1. Josephson Institute, "The Ethics of American Youth: 2008" (Los Angeles: Josephson Institute, 2009); http://charactercounts.org/programs/reportcard/index.html.

Chapter 27: Gambling

1. Chad Hills, "Childhood and Adolescent Gambling" (Colorado Springs, CO: Focus on the Family Action, n.d.); http://www.citizenlink.org/FOSI/gambling/A000002175.cfm.

Chapter 31: Occult Fascination

1. James Walker, "What Is the Occult?" *Watchman Expositor*, Vol. 9, No. 8 (1992).

Chapter 32: Pornography

1. National Coalition for the Protection of Children and Families, *What Every Parent Needs to Know About Addressing the Sexualized Culture* (Cincinnati, OH: National Coalition for the Protection of Children and Families, n.d.), 11.

2. Liz Perle, quoted in Anastasia Goodstein, *Totally Wired* (New York: St. Martin's Griffin, 2007), 104.

Chapter 33: Drug or Alcohol Abuse

1. David Walsh, *Why Do They Act This Way?* (New York: Free Press, 2004), 148.

2. Ibid.

3. Ibid., 142–44.

4. Sara Trollinger with Mike Yorkey, *Unglued & Tattooed* (Washington, DC: LifeLine Press, 2001), 30–31.

5. Center for Disease Control, "Morbidity and Mortality Weekly Report," Vol. 57, No. 45 (Washington, DC: Department of Health and Human Services, 2008), 1227; http://www.cdc.gov/mmwr/PDF/wk/mm5745.pdf.

6. Ibid., 1228.

7. American Cancer Society, "Cigarette Use Among Teens Inches Downward" (Atlanta: American Cancer Society, 2001); http://www.cancer.org/docroot/NWS/content/NWS_1_1x_Cigarette_Use_Among_Teens_Inches_Downward.asp.

8. Ibid.

9. Marijuana Addiction Treatment, "Marijuana Use Statistics"; http://www.marijuanaaddictiontreatment.org/statistics-facts.html.

10. See National Institute on Drug Abuse, "Research Report: Marijuana Abuse"

(Bethesda, MD: National Institutes of Health, July 2005); http://www.nida.nih.gov/
PDF/RRMarijuana.pdf.

11. Walsh, *Why Do They Act This Way?*, 148.

12. For this section see Jeff VanVonderen, *Good News for the Chemically Dependent and Those Who Love Them*, rev. and updated ed. (Nashville: Thomas Nelson, 1991), 21–22.

Chapter 34: Gossip

1. Rosalind Wiseman, *Queen Bees & Wannabes* (New York: Three Rivers Press, 2002), 112.

Chapter 41: Violence

1. See Douglas A. Gentile, "Video Games Affect the Brain—for Better and Worse," The Dana Foundation, July 23, 2009; http://www.dana.org/news/cerebrum/detail.aspx?id=22800.

Chapter 42: Sexual Activity

1. The Medical Institute, "What Is Meant by Consistent Condom Use?" 2008; http://www.medinstitute.org/public/123.cfm.

2. For the three God-given inner needs, see Lawrence J. Crabb Jr., *Understanding People: Deep Longings for Relationship*, Ministry Resources Library (Grand Rapids: Zondervan, 1987), 15–16; Robert S. McGee, *The Search for Significance*, 2nd ed. (Houston, TX: Rapha, 1990), 27–30.

3. For more information, visit National Coalition for the Protection of Children and Families, www.nationalcoalition.org.

4. *Merriam-Webster's Collegiate Dictionary*, electronic edition, s.v. "virgin," 2001.

5. Chuck Colson, "Lord, Make Me Chaste . . . Later!" *BreakPoint*, July 1, 2000; http://www.breakpoint.org/commentaries/13349-lord-make-me-chastelater.

6. For information on STDs see Centers for Disease Control, Sexually Transmitted Diseases Fact Sheets (Atlanta: Centers for Disease Control, n.d.), http://www.cdc.gov/std/healthcomm/fact_sheets.htm.